D0893251

# TWO AND TWENTY

# TWO AND TWENTY

How the Masters of Private Equity Always Win

## SACHIN KHAJURIA

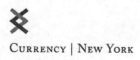

CURRENCY | NEW YORK

Published in the United States by Currency,
an imprint of Random House,
a division of Penguin Random House LLC, New York.

Currency and its colophon are trademarks
of Penguin Random House LLC.

Library of Congress Cataloging-in-Publication Data

Names: Khajuria, Sachin, author.
Title: Two and twenty / Sachin Khajuria.
Description: First edition. | New York: Currency, [2022]
Identifiers: LCCN 2022000916 (print) | LCCN 2022000917 (ebook) |
ISBN 9780593239599 (hardcover; alk. paper) | ISBN 9780593239605 (ebook)
Subjects: LCSH: Private equity. | Venture capital. | Finance.
Classification: LCC HG4751 .K5185 2022 (print) | LCC HG4751 (ebook) |
DDC 332.6—dc23/eng/20220302
LC record available at lccn.loc.gov/2022000916
LC ebook record available at lccn.loc.gov/2022000917

Printed in the United States of America on acid-free paper

crownpublishing.com

1st Printing

First Edition

Frontispiece image by Maxiphoto/iStock

Book design by Fritz Metsch

*For my father—the Man in the Arena*

It is not the critic who counts; not the man who points out how the strong man stumbles or where the doer of deeds could have done them better. The credit belongs to the man who is actually in the arena, whose face is marred by dust and sweat and blood; who strives valiantly; who errs, who comes short again and again, because there is no effort without error and shortcoming; but who does actually strive to do the deeds; who knows great enthusiasms, the great devotions; who spends himself in a worthy cause; who at the best knows in the end the triumph of high achievement, and who at the worst, if he fails, at least fails while daring greatly, so that his place shall never be with those cold and timid souls who neither know victory nor defeat.

—THEODORE ROOSEVELT, "Citizenship in a Republic"

# Contents

# Preface

Two percent in annual fees. Twenty percent of the profits. These are the fees private equity firms charge investors to manage and invest their money. The firms earn fees for running the cash they are entrusted with, and they also earn a share of the resulting profits from investments. This "Two and Twenty" formula sits at the core of the private equity industry, and although there are variations of it across firms and funds, it is the industry benchmark. It's an incentive that has helped create tremendous wealth for these dealmakers, while aligning the objectives of those who take the risk to put up the capital and those who seek to make profits from it on their behalf. In the simplest terms, the more money the investors make, the more the professionals make. They can both win together.

Today, private equity—in combination with other forms of private capital—is a $12 trillion industry.* It doubled in size during the 2010s, and by the end of this decade, it could well exceed $20 trillion. At the most basic level, what private equity does is invest money into an operating enterprise, a real business (or

---

*Throughout this book I use the simple unifying term "private capital" to refer to private equity as well as related alternative asset investment strategies managed by many private equity firms, including credit, real estate, natural resources, infrastructure, and growth equity. The principles in this book apply to all of these investment strategies, the most famous of which is private equity.

business plan) that needs to be fixed or that requires capital to grow, and then improve it before exiting at a profit. Put like that, it sounds simple. Private equity professionals pierce the veil, going beyond merely weighing the pros and cons of trading securities to understanding the workings of the underlying enterprise itself, just like a good company CEO would. Moreover, through the size of their investments, typically a controlling stake, private equity firms act like engaged owners, not passive investors. They eat what they cook. And that makes all the difference.

We cannot overestimate the reach of private equity across the global economy at this point. It is present nearly everywhere, in sectors as diverse as chemicals, energy and power, banks and insurance, consumer and retail, aerospace and government, manufacturing and industrials, media and telecommunications, leisure and entertainment, healthcare and pharmaceuticals, and technology. It has invested in subsectors we might not think of as natural habitats for Wall Street, from our children's schools to food storage to dating applications to family-ancestry tracing to military and intelligence technology. The vehicles used to make these investments are dizzying in their variety, from the traditional private equity funds that raise capital once and draw down commitments as required, to publicly listed funds, to the burgeoning class of funds that keep going without a finite life (so-called "permanent" or "perpetual" capital), to special-purpose vehicles funded on a one-off basis by pension funds and other investors or the balance sheets of private equity firms. There are hundreds of established private equity firms and hundreds more newer ones behind them. New firms crop up every year or two. At the apex of the industry sit a dozen major firms, the biggest of which are publicly listed, such as Blackstone and its rivals Carlyle and KKR. It's all too easy to get lost in the maze.

Blackstone manages over $875 billion in assets across investment strategies. Some firms are open about their desire to manage over a trillion dollars in assets themselves within just a few years. Taken together, the largest publicly listed firms manage over $2.5 trillion in assets. And even though the size of funds under management seems enormous, it underestimates the purchasing power of each firm, because of the multiplier effect of leverage. Money that is put to work in private equity funds can be leveraged by the debt raised on top of it to make investments. The unspent money in private equity funds, "dry powder" as we call it, can be multiplied by adding debt on top when investments are made. Take a relatively small fund, totaling $1 billion, and add $3 billion of debt. You now have $4 billion of purchasing power. Now consider not just private equity but all forms of private capital managed by private equity firms that can have debt raised on top of the money invested from the funds. That's trillions of dollars to invest.

Within our children's lifetimes, the industry could well be managing tens of trillions of dollars in assets. The field is huge and lucrative and has its fingers in nearly every sector of the economy, and yet the average person scarcely thinks about it—or would be able to explain how the industry works. Consider this: When we talk about private equity capital, we are, to a substantial extent, referring to money that belongs to the retirees of tomorrow. We are talking about individuals who rely—via their pension fund managers—on an industry they probably don't understand very well to deliver the returns they will need to live off in old age. We are talking about tens of millions of workers—employees like teachers, firefighters, and other pensioners around the world.

The rise of private equity has been hiding in plain sight. The industry doesn't mint the kind of high-publicity executives you find in "big tech" companies like Amazon or Tesla or Apple. But its reach is staggering. Investors turn to private equity to deliver higher, more consistent returns that are hard to get elsewhere. And as private equity firms introduce other strategies, such as credit, real estate, and infrastructure, these investors allocate money to those strategies too. The largest firms have become one-stop shops for alternative investments. Yet few outside Wall Street think much about them.

This knowledge asymmetry needs to change. It's time for people to learn what's really going on with private equity, to get to know the traits and motivations of the key people pulling the strings. That's where this book comes in.

We are all well conditioned to think about, talk about, and obsess about the "big banks" of Wall Street that were deeply involved in the chaos of the financial crisis of 2007–8. We are fixated with the "big tech" of Silicon Valley and its drumbeat of IPOs, not only because of those companies' insinuation into our daily lives but also due to the astronomical wealth that successful technology companies generate. Everyone with a 401(k) knows the alphabet soup of acronyms that cover names like Apple, Microsoft, Amazon, and Google. They know their retirement income relies on them. What about private equity? We know little about the handful of masters who control it or the people who work for them. This elite slice of society, with its strengthening grip on pensioners' money, has yet to be firmly established in the everyday lexicon. My goal in writing this book is to reveal the traits, culture, and temperament that fuel the most successful practitioners of Two and Twenty.

Two and Twenty as a fee concept is de rigueur across the industry, but there are striking differences in investment performance across private equity funds and firms. Even if the promised financial rewards are the same, some firms are able to consistently generate investment returns above what the mutual or index or exchange-traded fund (ETF) industries can provide far more cheaply, whereas others, over time, are beaten by the S&P 500 index of leading U.S. stocks. It is more than simply the promise of big payouts to investment professionals that makes many private equity firms excel and deliver excess returns for investors.

In the past two decades, private equity has supplanted investment banks and hedge funds in its allure—it's where the most talented young minds in finance go to make their mark. This is a people business, and the magic behind its success partly lies in how these people act and organize themselves to win. It's the individuals involved in private equity, their micro interactions, framed by the macro culture of the firms they work in. What drives a winning mindset is environment plus drive. In the chapters that follow, I will explore their motivations and the impact of their ambitions and beliefs on the deals they work on, the partnerships they create with the management teams in portfolio businesses invested in, and other stakeholders. When things go wrong, how and why does this happen? And what's the fix? I'll reveal that too.

By looking under the hood of private equity—and understanding the mindset of the folks involved—readers will better grasp why some funds (and firms) are more likely to work out than others. Whether you are a young person contemplating a career in private equity, a seasoned professional, or an armchair investor, this book will, I hope, both inform and entertain. My goal is to arm you with the knowledge and insights you will need to navigate and better understand one of the business world's largest, fastest-growing, most influential, and most opaque realms.

Why should you trust me to be a guide through this maze? Trying to divine the dealmaking motivations within private equity is a tall order for most outside observers of the industry, even those with aspirations to work in private equity or with business and financial acumen. I have worked in this industry for twenty-five years, first as an investment banker and then as an investor at one of the major firms at the partner level. I am hugely supportive of this industry and invest actively in it across the major firms—for my own account. I am your insider, but I am also independent. I'm not interested in spin or corporate talk. I call it like it is.

In these pages, I've tried to plot a course through the substance behind Two and Twenty, going beyond the headlines about how many billionaires and multimillionaires the private equity industry has minted or how much tax they should be paying or what their personal conduct in or out of the office is like. My focus is the business, the dealmaking, what I have learned from the successful investment professionals I have known who have originated and executed the deals that beat the stock market, time and time again. They are the industry elite, and they got there because they keep on delivering for investors.

In each chapter that follows, I will explore a different facet of the private equity mindset, using fictitious sketches, putting events and interactions under the microscope to explore what they reveal about what working in private equity at the senior level is *really* like. Some of these sketches are inspired by real-life deals and events, ones that have stuck in my mind for good reason, but I have masked or changed certain details that need to remain private and are not relevant to the important themes at play. As I relate these sketches, my goal is to focus on the *stories* that these investments tell and extract the vital lessons that make them worth recounting.

The principles I highlight will add up to a kind of playbook: a guide to being successful working in private equity. It's these patterns of behavior that animate and breathe life into what is increasingly a fundamental part of our economic system—an industry that should be better understood, as it continues to play a vital role in our financial health.

I'm well aware that the words "private equity" can connote very good things for some and engender distaste in others. While my hope is to add positivity to the conversation about private capital, I've endeavored, as I look into the mirror of my industry, to always stay rational—and to tell it to you straight, warts and all.

I hope that, by the time you turn the final page, you will have gotten a vivid portrait of an industry I love being a part of—and that you will have gained a greater understanding of the increasingly major role this industry plays, globally, in funding society.

We stand a much better chance of improving what we understand.

# TWO AND TWENTY

# CHAPTER ONE

# The Best Game in Town

The world economy is broken. Underlying fissures created by subprime mortgage losses have cracked open, with a devastating effect on the global financial system. Ordinary citizens are staring down the barrel of an ugly recession. Unemployment is soaring, on an unshakable course to double digits, and homeowners are drowning in foreclosure. The Federal Reserve has slashed interest rates as a credit crunch grips. Governments are forced to turn to their tools of last resort: colossal stimulus measures and nationalization plans to save households and corporations. Then, a week after the U.S. government is forced to bail out mortgage backers Fannie Mae and Freddie Mac, the unthinkable happens: Lehman Brothers, a major investment bank, files for bankruptcy. It is the largest bankruptcy in history.

It is 2008.

Inside the oak-paneled boardroom on the thirty-seventh floor of the Seagram Building in Midtown Manhattan, eleven partners of a well-known private equity firm discuss these events, what might happen next, and how they can profit from the crisis. One of the firm's investors is a German retirement fund for state employees, where the average salary is thirty thousand euros per year. These government workers in Bavaria have no idea that there is an ultra-wealthy asset manager in New York working hard on their behalf. Right now the firm is hunting for a smart bargain in their hometown, Munich.

The Founder of the Firm sits at the head of the oval French walnut table that dominates the room. Ten chairs are arranged for the other partners to use. These seats are made of the same elegant wood as the table but without armrests. The Founder's chair is different. It is made of a titanium alloy, like the million-dollar staircase in the lobby of the Firm's offices, and it pivots and reclines with ease—more throne than seat. No one dares occupy it when the Founder is absent. The spotlights are so bright that they would not look out of place in an emergency room. Through the floor-to-ceiling windows, those assembled are able to survey the riches of Park Avenue, with its European boutiques and attractive layout, but with the world economy hanging in the balance, no one has the time to soak in the view.

It is 11:45 A.M., and the Founder's schedule since he woke up six hours ago has been packed: a short helicopter ride from his beachfront residence in the Hamptons to New York, a competitive hour of tennis with a high-seeded U.S. Open player, and, over a light breakfast in a private dining room at the Harvard Club, a review of current economic data with a member of the board of the Federal Reserve.

The Founder has been a billionaire since his early forties. He is calm and assured, and he starts to talk to the room—to no one in particular and at the same time to all those assembled. His tone is soft, and his words are precise. His manner is awkward but commandingly so, a mix of deep experience and palpable threat. He leans forward as he speaks, resting his manicured hands on the yellow legal notepads and thick printouts of Excel models that cover the boardroom table in front of him. He dispenses his views with conviction, without hesitation or emotion, as if they are statements of fact rather than opinion. In over thirty years, he has lost money on deals just twice, and he displays the rarefied confidence of one who has earned the respect of others—even of his enemies. Amid the social and economic catastrophe raging outside the Firm, while everybody is preoccupied and nobody is watching, he is considering a new investment.

"I've seen this movie before," he says. "Europe is a few short months behind the U.S. They will get hit hard—I think extremely hard—and they won't know what hit them until it's too late. We finalize our preparations to buy soon, because the price of these securities will be in free fall. Let's get ready."

Although the facial expressions of his colleagues are stone-cold, like the air in the building, they know the Founder is right. His partners at the Firm and the fifteen midlevel and junior executives sitting at the outer edge of the room digest the Founder's order and plot the micro steps of how to execute it. Their eyes are sharp and their heads are turned, making sure they catch every nuance and gesture from the Founder as if they were made of pure gold. Everyone is wearing bespoke suits and expensive loafers, but the partners skip the ties. Three of the Firm's lawyers are writing down notes off to the side, and their presence and occasional advice confers upon the discussion the privacy and confidentiality benefits of attorney-client privilege.

This is the Firm's investment committee, the decision-making body made up of the partners as voting members and the rest of the Firm as observers and commentators. The committee meets every Monday, without fail, at 10:00 A.M. Eastern Time. For the last ninety minutes, the committee has torn apart the analysis contained in a forty-six-page investment memo for this prospective deal carefully put together by a deal team of three investment professionals. The team toiled around the clock for ten days to assemble the memo. This involved feedback calls on the last draft with each of the partners, as well as soliciting guidance from the Founder, before circulating a final version a few nights before. The investment memo contains concise inputs and exhaustive appendices from consultants, accountants, and lawyers, and finance terms from Wall Street's biggest banks, but it is the committee's dispassionate analysis of the deal that will drive the decision whether to proceed.

That judgment rests on the quality of replies to searing questions put to the deal team as a unit by the partners and a calibrated weighing up of whether the Firm's investors will be adequately compensated for the risks of the bet. Whether it's worth proceeding.

Over the weekend, the deal team fielded last-minute inquiries from every member of the committee. Some of the incoming commentary was hostile and cut open weaknesses in their work, meaning they would need to pull another all-nighter to prepare an addendum to the memo. Some feedback was encouraging and gave them confidence ahead of the meeting. Taken together, the input was meant to help the group get to the right answer about next steps, whether to proceed and, if so, on what terms. This is the birthing process of a private equity deal—a process designed to reveal the truth of the investment question at hand. But given the Founder's remarks, the iterative calculus of *do or don't do* is over—the approval to commit has been given in the guise of a friendly suggestion. The deal team must be ready to enter the market and buy quickly, without fear. It is time to be ruthless.

The target is called TV Corp, the largest free-to-air TV and radio broadcaster in Germany. The company was formerly owned by the Firm and is now publicly listed; vast files of information on the business and its competitors sit in the Firm's archives. What's more, the Firm has kept an eye on the company even after selling it off. Every quarter since exiting the business three years ago, the Firm's analysts have collected operating and financial data from relevant sectors of the economy, such as advertising and Hollywood movies, and processed them into financial models. Friendly senior corporate executives provide timely commentary on what is happening on the shop floor in TV and radio broadcasting, helping to ensure that the Firm is well-informed on significant facts and trends that are relevant to TV Corp. The information set is also enriched by deals the Firm has analyzed but not closed in adjacent sectors of the economy or in neighboring markets, either because the terms were not right or because a rival beat the Firm to it. This includes potential investments in TV and radio stations in France and in Scandinavia, possible deals involving broadcast towers in the UK, and the failed acquisition of a consumer goods company in northern Europe that would advertise on channels such as those TV Corp runs.

And so, by staying current, by keeping abreast even after the first investment in the target is long gone, the Firm can analyze everything relevant to the company's fortunes *going forward* in real time—from how much Procter & Gamble will spend on commercials for shampoo to the cost of screening Hollywood blockbusters to the reaction of trade unions and politicians to job cuts and restructurings. The data and the Firm's history with the target have tipped the scales in the Firm's favor. The Founder is in a strong position to make an audacious move on the company again—this time during a global economic earthquake, when nobody else is paying attention.

Last time, the Firm's investors doubled their investment in

TV Corp—every dollar put in turned into two dollars on the way out. This time, the objective is for the investment to be even more lucrative. The goal is to buy the public stock at a discount of over seventy-five percent from the price at which the Firm sold the very same shares last time, and to buy the private debt issued by TV Corp at less than a third of its original value. These prices would be at severely distressed levels, making the purchases highly opportunistic and likely to be enormously profitable when financial markets recover—as long as the business remains solvent and weathers the financial crisis. Or, in the parlance of private equity, as long as the investment is "money good." As long as it survives.

Ordinarily, the Firm would look to make investments in private companies, not publicly traded securities. Buy the target, control it, improve it, and sell it for a profit. What is striking is that in this case, with financial markets cracking and investor sentiment at such a low, the Firm is expertly prepared to act. It's actually a great time for the Firm to capture the opportunity, even though the investment is in listed stock and debt rather than acquiring a business outright. This is a target the Firm knows. It's a scenario that the partners feel can't go wrong—at the right price—and that the investment professionals can model with reasonable confidence. Mutual funds, index funds, and ETFs are running out the door, sending the prices of these securities into free fall. Passive money is trying to escape. Meanwhile, the active managers in the room want to back up the truck and buy in bulk at a big discount.

Why are the prices of these securities so distressed? The world is in chaos. Global demand for advertising on TV is plummeting because the multinationals are worried about the financial crisis causing a hit to their revenues. Everything that once looked essential, from cars to consumer products to bank accounts, is being re-sorted into two buckets—what needs to exist and what doesn't. The markets do not wait for reality to catch up; they act faster, anticipating the impact on companies that are likely to be sensitive to the shock. And so, even if you and I think it's unlikely that everyone in Germany will stop buying basic household goods, or that they might delay buying a new car but won't likely cancel the decision to purchase, or that they might need an incentive to upgrade their movie and sports channel package but won't stop watching—the truth is, nobody knows for sure, especially when it looks like the Earth might stop spinning on its axis. It's one thing to talk about it in hindsight; it is another to bet millions of other people's dollars on it while in the eye of the storm, not knowing how bad the storm will be. It takes experts armed with know-how and data. It takes the experts at the Firm.

If the gamble pays off, the Firm's investors will be thrilled. Why? Put simply, they now rely on private equity firms to manage their money. People are living longer and the global population is increasing, and with these demographic trends come political and social imperatives to maintain pension entitlements and to invest wisely for retirees. To keep producing retirement income. Sovereign wealth funds, high-net-worth families, and large college endowments need to preserve and grow assets for the benefit of future generations. They cannot afford to get it wrong.

Consider, for example, a retirement system for public sector employees that consistently needs annual investment returns of around seven percent. To receive these returns, the pension program is compelled to look beyond passive money investors that track the stock market or invest in government bonds as attractive and safe places to house the money. Mutual funds, index funds, and ETFs might cut it for one year or over a run of years, but such instruments often encounter volatile periods during which the returns are negative or insufficient. That's not good enough to build a retirement around. Pension money needs high, stable returns through the ups and downs of the market and business cycles. It needs the returns that private equity keeps delivering to investors.

The best private equity funds minimize risk while delivering annual returns in excess of, say, fifteen percent—with the top firms generating even higher returns while presiding over very few investments that fail to work out. And so teachers, firefighters, healthcare workers, and other employees who are part of retirement systems depend on private equity to make the math of their pensions work. They need places like the Firm.

Once the Firm's investment committee meeting is complete, the TV Corp deal team regroups in the office of the partner in charge of the project. They review their notes, decide what follow-up might be required, and finalize an execution plan involving the stock and bond traders who will place the buy orders in the market to acquire the securities at the approved prices. They will be careful to "stage" their purchases so as not to move the market upward, to stay under the radar. By the time their private equity rivals figure out that owning TV Corp's securities is a compelling trade-off of return versus risk, it will be too late. The Firm will have gotten there first, and the prices will already have started to rise, meaning that the Firm will be sitting on freshly made gains within a matter of days. The Firm's carefully choreographed investment will eventually turn heads on trading screens, with copycat investors piling into similar positions for fear of missing out—only to increase the Firm's gain. At least that is the plan the deal team has.

Fast-forward twelve months, and the monetary and fiscal weapons that the world's central banks and governments let rip in response to the economic vortex of the times have resulted in the securities in the Firm's shopping basket tripling in value. The Firm's funds had acquired a blend of the TV Corp's public stock as well as its debt.

So what do you think the Founder does next? He urges his colleagues that now is the right time to exit, because the incremental risk of holding on to these securities significantly outweighs the further reward they can gain. There is little juice left in the markets to squeeze. Every day you don't sell, you are buying, as the saying in private equity goes.

At this point, of course, they are right to cash in their chips— you and I probably would too—and by doing so within a few weeks, in an orderly and quiet manner, the Firm exits the investment and thus makes its investors three times their money in little over a year. A private equity fund put in a hundred million dollars, and three hundred million dollars came out. In this situation, the Firm did not need to acquire the target outright— its quick flip of liquid securities in TV Corp was driven by a combination of being informed about the business as a former owner, staying up to date on the company, and having the smarts and iron will to strike when the financial markets plunged.

That's not something an index-tracking fund can do.

I highlight this deal because it shows how private equity can be a serial investor, a flexible investor, and a decisive investor even during a time of severe economic dislocation. Ordinarily, private equity would have bought the target outright, or perhaps lent money to it or provided growth capital. But in this case, private equity balanced the unknowns of trying to acquire a business it used to own with the immediate liquid opportunity of buying pieces of it at reduced rates during a crisis. The crisis was a meltdown in the financial markets, but it could be any crisis—such as a pandemic—that creates the opportunity to deploy investors' money smartly. It can be any kind of edge.

The investment service provided by private equity firms to investors is fast becoming essential, but unlike an essential utility, it isn't charged at some kind of regulated rate. Two and Twenty means that if a private equity deal works out, the investment professionals will get a bumper payday for producing bumper results. The private equity firm will retain twenty percent of the deal's profits and share them among its employees—usually, with the more senior members taking the most. Some firms tie profit distributions for investment professionals exclusively to the deals they work on; others give investment professionals a slice of profits from all deals in the funds they are investing. It varies. The important point is that there's a huge incentive to make the deal profitable for investors.

Consider this: Although the private equity firm takes a twenty percent cut of profits, the money at risk belongs to the investors. The investment professionals will usually invest alongside their clients out of their own pockets, but in the aggregate, the sum total of their money amounts to only a small percentage (for example, two to five percent) of the capital invested. So it's only a fraction of the capital at risk. The vast majority of the money at risk is other people's money, but the slice of return that private equity takes home comes from everyone's money. This agreed-upon symbiosis between the firms and their investors is central to the financial incentives at the heart of private equity.

This arrangement is standard and accepted, and it works well for investors in private equity funds most of the time. The incentives are a big part of why private equity folks deliver, for the risk they take with their own money is outweighed by the return they can reap if their deals for investors succeed.

Of course, to pull off private equity deals, the investment professionals behind them need not only superior information but also tremendous skill. And behind this skill lie the culture and DNA of these individuals—and the principles and traits that animate them as top dealmakers. It is what propels them to the one percent of the economic pyramid. Private equity is the envy of Wall Street, the place to be for those aspiring to become good investors.

If it were easy, anybody could do it. Private equity folks are always running multiple deals like the one in our sketch at the same time. Weekly investment committee meetings often cover a handful of deals in detail, as well as updates on several more. It isn't easy to originate, execute, and make a success of projects that can be diverse in industry, structure, complexity, and geography. How they do it, and do it consistently, is worth understanding. These are the people that make pension systems work.

Every week, private equity professionals might look at a storied public company they would like to take private during hard times, where a once-convincing narrative has fallen out of favor in unhospitable public markets and some heavy lifting needs to be done far from the limelight. Or a growing business in the digital economy that needs money to expand. Or a carve-out of an unloved division of a stodgy conglomerate. Or a niche opportunity to put money to work in a specialized field of life sciences or technology or natural resources. Or a hungry, acquisitive platform that needs capital to fuel its war chest for more bolt-ons and tuck-ins. Or even a big, transformative transaction that would create an industry leader. There are more deal choices than you could reasonably list.

To gain its edge, the private equity firm considering these deals might have the inside track via prior ownership of a competing business, or relationships with management or the board of directors, or expertise in the supply or customer chain of the ecosystem around the investment. The masters of private equity have plenty of angles. The investment committees are experienced and nimble enough to duck and weave through each idea within hours, assigning next steps for the project teams and making decisions worth hundreds of millions or billions of dollars of investors' cash, from entry into an investment to refinancing it to selling out several years later.

It's now early 2022, nearly fourteen years since the original events that inspired the TV Corp sketch. The impact of the financial crisis has given way to another global shock, the Covid-19 pandemic. But the private equity industry has thrived, growing at double-digit rates, raising larger funds, and making far more profit for its investors and itself than anyone could have imagined. A firm once managing billions of dollars has its eyes on tens of billions; those once managing tens of billions are now managing hundreds of billions. A handful of firms are rapidly approaching a trillion dollars under management each.

What counts most about these firms, of course, is not only their growing size but their performance in deals, and not just in private equity but across all the forms of private capital they manage. The force with which the financial crisis, and now the pandemic, rattled the economy and financial markets provided just the kind of rupture that the masters of private equity are conditioned to maneuver to their advantage. They leap into the void created by crises, taking the lowest risk they can in order to make the highest return for their investors. When other investors are frozen with indecision or (even worse) pull out, private equity looks at jumping into the chasm. Private equity figures it's worth it to make something of the uncertainty, and sees lucrative opportunities where most of us just see danger.

The masters of private equity move deftly, placing bets in this corner of the world, then that one. They aim to be agile when selecting new investments across sectors, to be open-minded about investing in the equity in one situation and in the debt in another, and to be meticulous when planning for critical success factors, from the tax structures of their funds to the hiring of executives at portfolio companies. They have the financial muscle to navigate through the worst recessions. Sometimes, their investments can fail—but the private equity firm will still survive.

Massive scale has also made private equity's profits massively more attractive for the professionals who work in the industry. We have talked about the twenty-percent cut of all profits on deals that a typical private equity fund charges its investors. We should also be clear about what happens to the two-percent management fees that are charged annually to investors to run their money. As with the profit share, there are variations across firms and funds, but two percent is an industry benchmark. It's what most firms aim for and most achieve when putting together investment funds. It's the industry norm.

At the dawn of the industry, in the latter stages of the last century, the management fees charged by private equity firms were only supposed to cover their running costs: to pay for employees, real estate, and other routine business expenses. As the industry has matured, these management fees have arguably become a source of profit, because the scale of the assets that private equity manages is so immense. In turn, this can create a big incentive to supersize.

Whether a private equity firm charges two percent across all of the funds it manages or other combinations of management fees and profit sharing in the different investment strategies that it runs for investors, the point is essentially the same. The greater the size of a firm's assets under management, the larger the pool of management fees. For the major private equity firms that manage multiple forms of private capital and are publicly listed, one of the key attractions to public market investors of their listed stock is the stability and growth of these management fees.

And think about it this way: The industry's rise, including its growing size, has only been possible because private equity investing really works. Most firms deliver the range of returns they pitch, even after charging Two and Twenty. Performance is the principal reason that investors keep coming back, that new investors are attracted, and that the industry is set to continue to expand aggressively, not only in size but also in the breadth of the private capital permutations that the major firms manage. It works. This growth is incredible when you consider the cut taken and the fees clipped, which in dollars-and-cents terms are mind-blowing in scale to the ordinary workers whose pensions or sovereign wealth assets, or the students and teachers whose educational institutions' endowments, are entrusted in part to private equity firms to manage.

What is also true is that private equity firms have entered the white space created in the financial system where others have left the stage. Take, for example, private equity firms moving into providing credit directly to institutions. Following the financial crisis, traditional lenders such as banks faced rising capital requirements and more onerous regulation (as might be expected, as part of the authorities' attempts to avoid another crisis). As a direct result, they started to retreat from traditional credit activities, often hoarding cash. This deliberate exit left the door open for private equity firms and their debt funds to take up the slack, fueling the provision of credit from these nontraditional sources, which are often called "shadow banks."

Private capital funds investing in credit, which are arguably less regulated than banks and can be as opaque as private equity funds, now represent a very significant part of the assets under management for the major firms. These private equity firms have not only ventured into this white space, they've captured it with both hands. Another big example of private capital growth is infrastructure investing, where private equity firms have stepped into the shoes of governments to acquire, finance, and manage real assets such as airports, toll roads, and utility companies.

Credit and infrastructure funds feature heavily as forms of private capital managed by the major private equity firms, alongside buying and selling businesses in the private equity funds. And as with private equity, moving into these areas has worked well, because the investment returns being delivered are consistent and attractive to retirement systems and other investors.

The larger private equity firms manage several investment vehicles across many forms of private capital under one roof. At many firms, the founders—just a handful of individuals—still either own or control the majority of the firm. However, at the major firms, especially the publicly listed ones, enormous steps have been underway in recent years to transition to a more institutional structure like that of a corporation.

Even at these largest firms, however, the circle of the most senior investment professionals (who often have the title of "partner," "member," or an equivalent corporate title) is tight, relative to the enormous size of assets under management. A private equity fund sized at, say, ten billion dollars might have twenty partners running it, if that. If the next fund for the same firm is sized at twenty billion dollars, it's likely that the same investment committee will preside over it, and it's also likely that the partnership circle won't double—it might increase to, say, thirty partners, or fewer—and most of the increase will be from internal promotions up the ranks, along with a couple of lateral hires. A private equity firm's structure has to be tight-knit, even as assets under management grow materially, in order to remain decisive and nimble, to maintain the culture and know-how. And keeping the culture and know-how of the firm central to how the investment professionals invest is vital.

With investment performance stable and strong, a clear realization has set in across the financial world: Private equity firms are the place to be. They attract and keep many of the finest investors, drawn from business, finance, and industry—using the twin magnets of opportunity and reward to reel them in across private equity and other forms of private capital. A decade ago, an accomplished credit investing team might consider a lateral move from one bank to another, say from JP Morgan to Goldman Sachs; today, the brightest want to work at Blackstone, the largest firm, or its primary competitors, like Carlyle and KKR.

These investment superstars deliver performance gains to the private capital funds, so more money floods in from investors, so more cash needs to be invested, and that means teams need to grow and hire—and so the cash carousel goes around.

It's a people business. The people who work in private equity make the industry what it is and make it work. Private equity is not just about the active management of assets; it is about the hyperactive control of investments—whether the deals involve outright voting control of a company, or a minority stake, or lending to a business, or buying and managing infrastructure. And this control is led by people, by the investment professionals who run deals from entry to exit.

There is nothing automated about it. It's not something that a supercomputer can do or artificial intelligence can replace. Success or failure on deals is not about a system or an investment process; it is about the people in control, the people who make the daily decisions. These people have proven that they possess a heightened ability to filter everything through the lens of risk versus return, to analyze the upside versus the downside, to put the band of likely outcomes for an investment in the spotlight. These are people who have the appetite and stamina to stick to a deal for a horizon as long as a decade of their lives, people who are prepared to run marathons for a pot of gold at the end.

In private equity, capitalism has perfected its version of a virtuous circle. It is an essential service for pension funds and other investors. It draws in the best people. It performs consistently. It is growing rapidly. And in a pandemic or other world crisis, when liquid markets whipsaw and look uncertain, the illiquid nature of private equity and other forms of private capital—the inability to take your money out whenever you want—can be oddly appealing. In a volatile market, private equity is one of the last hopes investors have. It is more expensive and more opaque than other types of investing, but it works.

That's why private equity is the best game in town.

How do private equity experts ascend the ranks to sit at the power table of the investment committee? How do they think and operate? What are their core beliefs? What drives them to succeed? Why do they take on this demanding job? What systemic problems and nuances must they navigate—and can they be fixed? In the chapters that follow, I will paint an insider's picture of private equity, unvarnished, taking one brushstroke at a time.

Let's start with the secret sauce that private equity is selling.

# CHAPTER TWO

# We Don't Sell Plain Vanilla

What private equity sells sounds so good, some think it's alchemy—the financial equivalent of turning water into wine. We always beat the market; we're better than a random walk. We generate high returns over the long term and minimize the risk of losing money. We focus on the endgame, not the myopia of quarterly or annual results. We add value to your investments in a way that very few others can. We see opportunities others can't see or can't handle. Your money will be locked up with us, but in a few years, you will get a multiple of it back—without any effort from you. Trust us: Hand it over.

This premise is in striking contrast to the modus operandi of other asset managers. The masters of private equity do not pick stocks or bonds in liquid markets and hope to ride a rising wave of positive sentiment. They do not spread their investors' money thinly around to achieve diversification across the financial markets. They aren't long some stocks and short others. They are not seeking to replicate the S&P 500 index. There are no chartists or research gurus. Investing passively in an ETF, like those managed by BlackRock or Vanguard, might mean paying a yearly management fee equivalent to ten basis points (0.1 percent)—if that—and you keep all of the investment performance for yourself; it is not typically shared with the asset manager. In contrast, private equity is pitched as a premium rate service at Two and Twenty. The difference is stark.

Typically, a private equity deal involves a fund buying a controlling interest in a business, or at least making a sizable enough investment to have significant influence, and along with this role comes one or more seats on the board of directors—or control of the board, including the appointment of the chair. The operating business could be an established company or a growing start-up or a division carved out of a larger group. It could also be a public company taken off the stock market by the private equity fund in a leveraged buyout, using high-yield debt to finance the acquisition.

Once the transaction is complete, the deal team that led the investment gets involved with the management team of the company to make the business more valuable, to make it attractive to sell a few years down the road. Typically, the same deal team lives with the investment from entry to sale. They might be supplemented with additional resources, such as industry experts that the firm also employs, and they will certainly work intensively with the other non-executives on the board of the target they've invested in. The mix of people assembled in this way by private equity will be financiers and operating executives. They don't disappear once the deal is done—they are not there for the initial glory of "doing a deal"—and in any event, for them the big payout will come when the investment is disposed of, or, in private equity parlance, when the gain in value "crystallizes."

The improvement in the business can be an overhaul, a house-cleaning and transformation of strategy from the inside out, or a more targeted approach to address a specific set of issues. It can be the execution of a strategic vision to grow the company, such as by making acquisitions or adding new product lines. These improvements frequently involve changes in the target's management, usually with the help of industry experts who often serve on the board of directors and its key committees.

The exit from the investment can be the sale (partial or full) to a large corporation or another private equity fund, or a listing (or relisting) on the stock market, after which point the private equity fund would "sell down" its stock in an orderly fashion over a period of months. Or it can be a combination of these approaches. The investment can be refinanced once or multiple times by adding more debt to the business as its earnings improve, or by borrowing against the value of the investment before it is exited, returning some of the investors' money early. Sometimes, part of the target is sold off earlier than the rest of the business; if keeping it doesn't fit with the business plan for the investment, better to dispose of it to a bidder who sees more value in it. These are all forms of what in the industry is called "realization"—that is, getting the money out and distributing it.

There are countless combinations of these ingredients in the life cycle of an investment, and limitless permutations when it comes to sequencing events. The recipe can vary. What is constant is that the masters of private equity have a deep understanding of both the financial side and the operating side of a situation—and it is this 360-degree awareness of all the angles that allows them to spot opportunity, whether that clever investment is buying the company outright or making a critical loan to fix a business's financing hole, or developing the real estate or infrastructure assets of the target. It is this vision, this instinct to discern the moment to strike and the understanding of how to execute that strike, that is at the heart of what makes private equity special. It's pressing the right buttons at the right time to make the investment more valuable.

None of this is straightforward or static. Analyzing a business's operations involves understanding the supply and demand in the sector, the competitive landscape over time, the impact of technology, and the evolution of regulation, as well as which levers can be pulled to create value. How resilient is the business to a downturn? How robust is the capital structure? What is the opportunity to refinance the debt? What is the long-term strategic vision of the company that we will be *selling to someone else* in five years' time? How realistic and believable—how sellable—is that vision? Interrogating the operations in this way requires specialist knowledge and a deep understanding of the management team of the target and their motivations. Building powerful networks across each industry they invest in is a must for the masters of private equity. They are not day-to-day executives—they rely on excellent management, and therefore they have to know what excellent management looks like.

The operating and financial lenses that private equity professionals use to analyze a target overlap, and it is critical in private equity to add those two halves together and look at the business as a whole. The capital structure and financing must go hand in hand with the strategic vision and the execution of operations. Once the total picture is clear, the investment professionals run a battery of spreadsheet scenarios to stress-test the company and consider which cases for the target would be prudent to include as part of a baseline model for the investment. In one case, for example, revenues grow quickly in some product lines, but others are discontinued as they are a drag on profitability. In other cases, there is a labor cost problem or a supply chain squeeze, or capital expenditures run over budget. Dozens of scenarios—if not more—are run, and then distilled to narrow the scenario down to a realistic "base case" for a deal.

At each stage of the investment process, from originating a deal to making it happen to selling years down the road, private equity focuses hard on the quality of the management team on whom they will rely to deliver a more valuable business than the one they started with. It is through partnering with management that what is discussed by the investment committee in a boardroom is put into practice on the shop floor. Investment professionals are expected to be in regular contact with their allocated counterparts at the company—be it the CFO or the CEO or the respective working groups of target executives—as well as the other non-executive board members. It's essential for private equity to have a feel for how the management team is doing, what their fears and hopes during the lifetime of the investment are, and how private equity can best assist in turning theoretical ideas into tangible value. This entire process is dynamic and iterative and comprises a vital part of the private equity job. And it requires empathy and emotional IQ as well as trusted, authentic multiyear relationships, in good times and in less good times for the deal, between the investment professionals and the target's executives. Such traits are not always found on Wall Street.

Although well-performing investment professionals in other fields of asset management, such as the hedge fund and mutual fund industries, regularly conduct their own versions of this work, it is in private equity that it finds its most thorough and compelling form. From the outside, it can look to the public a little like the dark arts, like magic that surely must have a catch. In reality, there is no mystique about it. The folks who work in private equity are simply very good investors, and the firms harness the skills of these professionals into a collective setting to drive the best returns. Every hire must be additive; every new seat must help grow the pie so that everyone's take-home bit of Two and Twenty is bigger.

How is this machine organized? In a compact manner that, a little like the formulas for fees, has largely remained consistent since the early, modest days of the industry. A private equity firm's organizational chart is a rough pyramid structure, with three broad groups of investment professionals: the analytical base, the middle layer, and the senior set, called the partners or managing directors, who are the individuals most directly responsible to investors for the firm's investment performance and conduct. If the firm's founder(s) still run the firm, of course, they sit at the top of this set.

The analytical base consists of young investment professionals whose job is to obtain a crisp and thorough understanding of the numbers and details behind the business model and the finances of an investment. They also help run a deal by directing critical workstreams as task masters, working in concert with lawyers, accountants, tax experts, and other consultants. Typically, these analytic foot soldiers are a couple of years out of a prestigious college—and many have had an entry-level tour of duty in the investment banking divisions of major Wall Street banks, such as Goldman Sachs, Morgan Stanley, or JP Morgan. Aspiring private equity masters can expect to spend up to five years at this end of the pyramid before moving up to the next rung: the middle layer, whose members serve as the day-to-day deal quarterbacks and are responsible for quality-control checks on the juniors' investment work.

The middle layer is the center of the private equity pyramid, and it consists of professionals who are generally in their late twenties to mid-thirties. They can play up and down the pyramid—for example, helping the analytical base to spread and interpret the numbers one moment and discussing with a partner what to pay the CEO who was hired or fired that week the next moment. Depending on the firm, in most cases this layer has been promoted from the junior layer after performing well and demonstrating they can step up effectively.

Moving up, the partners run the investment activities of their firm. They find deals and lead the execution of these opportunities. When the investment committee gathers to discuss deals, the partners typically speak first to summarize the situation, including what they think the investment committee should focus the discussion on. They are the elite investors of the firm; they bear the biggest burden for success or failure, and they typically earn the lion's share of the profits collected by the firm as Two and Twenty. They've made it.

Across different firms, of course, the number of titles involved in each stage of the ladder will vary. At one end of the spectrum, some firms resist having too many titles, preferring to stick to perhaps three, such as "Associate," "Principal," and "Partner," to cover the entire structure. For them, having too many titles diminishes the value of each one and subtly encourages employees to covet promotion too much.

At the other end of the spectrum, some firms prefer multiple titles for each stage of the ladder—for instance, maintaining a distinction between "Associate" and "Senior Associate" or "Vice President" and "Director" to separate individuals within the junior and middle ranks, respectively. Here, each aspiring private equity master must work through the larger promotion steps between the junior, middle, and senior ranks as well as the "mini-steps" within each rank.

What is consistent across firms, however, is that promotion is not guaranteed by tenure. There has to be a slot for you one level up for you to make it, and you have to earn it. The economics of moving up—more compensation for you, more of the Two and Twenty in your own pocket—must make sense for the firm and your colleagues too. You'll have to be able to grow the pie of economics for everyone, not just take a bigger slice of it. This dynamic is similar in other industries with a similar structure, such as at the best investment banks or some white-shoe law firms, but at Two and Twenty, of course, the economics at stake are much bigger. Partners can be worth hundreds of millions of dollars, with the founders worth billions. It's much rarer to find that in a bank or a law firm.

Lateral hires are rare, but they are becoming more common as private equity firms have grown and are venturing into new areas. For example, a firm that has never before invested in social impact investing or infrastructure or renewable energy or life sciences might create a team for each such vertical, recruiting laterally on the understanding that the members of the new team will work alongside a long-standing partner of the firm to ensure cultural continuity and a common approach to making investments. Otherwise, it is often thought that promoting from within can be a much safer bet than hiring from outside. That is part of why many of the senior lateral hires who have joined the industry or moved from one firm to another have specialist skills, such as originating deals in a new vertical or technical knowledge in that area that cannot be replicated from within their new firms. This trend is set to grow aggressively, as private equity firms continue to grow in other fields of private capital.

It is hard to believe, but it can take only three or four investment professionals to find, execute, and manage an investment worth billions of dollars. The lifeblood of a private equity firm, these deal teams generally consist of one employee from the analytical base, one from the middle layer, and one or two from the senior set. The average age of the deal team is in the midthirties. This isn't big law, where more lawyers and more associates means more billable hours to charge the client for. There may be only a handful of investment professionals for each billion dollars of investors' money under management. Some firms prefer bigger teams with fewer key tasks per person, but the major firms tend to be lean, which means that the profit shares from deals available to each team member tend to be the highest in the industry. In most firms, the idea is to maintain the same deal team on each investment from start to finish, although each investment professional is unlikely to work with the same group of colleagues on every deal. There may be employee turnover, and some roles may be partly carved out to dedicated groups such as a financing team or a team focused on operations, but ultimately the crucible of responsibility and economics will sit within a close circle. Inside this team, there is no room for partisan ideas or divisive politics. Everyone just wants a solid result on the investments they are responsible for. They're in it together.

Put differently, we can say that although private equity firms have the pyramid structure mentioned earlier, within a deal team the modes of working together every day are usually much flatter. Each level has its role, but it's not very formal. Doors are always open. Calls at nearly any hour are okay. Each deal team operates as a very tight working unit. If two partners work together on a deal, they are likely to differ in tenure—a younger partner who runs the project and an elder who is available for counsel. The idea is to encourage taking responsibility for both the part of the deal you are most focused on, such as the analytics for the junior layer, and the deal as a whole. It's natural to feel personally responsible for the deal on behalf of your investors. You'll want to be all over it.

So how do deal team members work together on a new investment to generate the deal alchemy? The fundamental elements of their interaction start with a clear line of sight from the confluence of events that have created the deal opportunity, whether it is idiosyncratic or thematic in nature, and continue down the path that the investment needs to take in order to make money. The best firms start with a shared vision and execution plan outlining why they want to do the deal and how they will make it work.

The thought process within an investment professional's mind as a potential deal nears goes something like this:

1. We believe that the following things can happen to this business, to its revenues and costs and cash flows and assets, whether it is already an established market player or it can (re) emerge to be one.

2. If we invest so much money in this or that way and make these changes to this company, partnering with these clever executives and hiring these experienced directors on the board, financed in this way and tax structured in that way, and then sell it with this story to someone else, we can generate returns between this lower and that upper bound within this time frame.

3. This bridge from the potential to the kinetic, from the price paid on day one to the range of valuations that can be achieved at exit, defines the possible growth trajectory in the investors' money during the life of the deal. This will be the journey we take for several years until this is achieved.

The deal team refines this lens several times during the life of an investment, primarily to sharpen the view of the outcome that can be achieved, as it digs further into the operations of the target and generates ideas for how to improve the financials. There are status updates for the investment committee or some subset thereof at least twice a year, and if the investment is challenged or is about to undergo a material event such as disposal of a business unit or the IPO of the company, or the hiring and firing of senior management, these debriefings are likely to be more frequent and conducted in greater depth. Of course, the input from colleagues will help the deal team refocus its lens on the investment and ideally lead to a better outcome for the investors and therefore for the private equity firm as well.

At every point, the team is obsessed with protecting the investment against capital loss and increasing the company's value to be in a position to capture more profit on the deal at the exit. The business plan results versus what was budgeted and the success of the company strategy versus what was underwritten are debated, with the target's management team, its board, and the investment committee as regular touch points. Issues are dissected and theses are reconstructed, with gaps in the thought process filled in with more work until the picture is credible and clear.

Inside this hive of activity, every investment professional is aligned, because the target outcome is to make money for investors—and for everyone to share in the spoils. The goal is to be very positive about doing deals where they make sense and even more negative about ill-conceived or ill-prepared deals. This is not venture capital. There's no sense in "Let's back a bunch of smart ideas with cash and brains, and some will work out big and others will flop and that is all okay." The idea is to have a strong chance of winning on every investment.

If the discussion in the investment committee on a new deal idea looks positive, the partners lean in to help the team get the project over the line, brainstorming about how to weight the deal's circumstances most heavily to the advantage of the firm. If the discussion is about a live investment and how it is tracking against what the deal team said when the investment was approved, when investors' dollars were committed, the firm will be rigorous about whether the deal is performing according to expectations, whether the numbers are interesting or alarming. The masters of private equity have perfected this formula of working such that there is little doubt or confusion over what they are seeking to achieve on investments.

Everyone is aligned around a common goal. Everyone knows what results are expected.

Let us pause here to look at a fictitious sketch inspired by a real-life situation.

It is 2017. Pharma Corp, once the darling of some of the smartest hedge fund investors and Wall Street bankers, has lost over eighty percent of its stock market value in the past twelve months, amounting to $100 billion of shareholders' money. The company owns the rights to, and manufactures, essential drugs for everyday medical conditions. Many of the drugs are household names. But the outlook for this storied company is bleak.

Everything that could have gone wrong with Pharma Corp has gone wrong. Its business model is centered on hoovering up scores of pharmaceutical drug acquisition targets, slashing their research and development budgets to the bone in order to boost cash flow, and implementing massive price hikes on its drugs for patients and their insurers. Whether this is legal is debatable. It's certainly an aggressive way to run a healthcare company.

U.S. lawmakers have accused the company of price goug-
ing. Its accounting policies have been compared to the likes of
Enron. When the company moved its headquarters from the
United States to the Cayman Islands, critics called the switch
a tax avoidance ploy. A handful of savvy investors have declared
the balance sheet unsustainable and its debt burden—from binge
after binge of leveraged acquisitions—as fatal. As a pharmaceutical business, the company's deprioritizing of science and inven-
tion looks distasteful, especially in the light of profligate company
expenditures like the purchase of a Gulfstream private jet for the
personal use of the CEO. The monopoly position on medicines
it has enjoyed for many medical conditions, with no generic,
unbranded drugs available as alternatives, now serves as a noose
rather than an advantage. Some stellar hedge funds, once entirely
confident in the company's stock, have lost big; in the case of one
such hedge fund, a billion dollars of investor money was wiped
out. And to top it all off, a Netflix documentary about Pharma
Corp has raised the damning specter of corruption in the form of
allegations by executives who have fled the struggling business.

Meanwhile . . . a few blocks from Central Park, on the fifty-
fifth floor of the Seagram Building, the Firm is three chess
moves ahead. . . .

It is just past noon, and the investment committee of the Firm
is firing questions at a seasoned partner and his deal team as if
they are gladiators fighting for their lives in the Colosseum. They
have been sparring for nearly two hours, and this is the second
and final audience for the team before a clear decision is to be
taken whether to pursue the potential deals they are discussing.

Over the past three years, the deal team has been exploring
how to invest profitably in the pharmaceuticals industry without
taking on the speculative risk of investing in the development of

new drugs for medical conditions. They do not want to compete with corporate giants in the space or university research departments, as they are not interested in a costly scientific arms race over new drug research. They have watched patiently as Pharma Corp, and others like it, raised the prices of several types of drugs, and they have wisely decided that investing in this price-driven strategy is not where they want to be. It is too risky. It lacks moral fiber.

Instead, the team has been hunting for niche opportunities in pharmaceuticals, an industry worth over a trillion dollars. There are bound to be some that fit the Firm's appetite for risk versus return. The partner has hired pharmaceutical veterans to help the Firm better understand the nuances of different ideas. Some of these hires will likely step in to join the management teams and boards after any deals are successfully closed. The team has attended scores of training sessions, industry conferences, and calls with experts. They have mined the data and sliced the operating and financial analysis along every axis they can think of. The team has iterated the operating models for individual pharmaceutical products for months and run financial models for various business cases, revealing potential returns as well as risks.

The deal team has brought in regulatory advisors to quantify the dangers of adverse changes in the rules. Technology advances are considered, such as the impact of telemedicine and new diagnostic tools on how often and how much certain drugs can be dispensed for particular medical conditions. The team analyzes qualitative shifts in consumer and competitor behavior. Operating cost structures for target companies under consideration are scrapped—and rebuilt from the ground up on a "zero budget" basis. Outsourcing contracts for manufacturing drugs and sales efforts are investigated. Successful and failed deals of rivals are dissected to identify why money was made or lost. Parallels and analogies are considered from other industries—for example, what other sectors have assets that generate recurring revenues, which can then be milked for more cash flow using better marketing efforts? Movie libraries? Music back catalogs?

The deal team has been cramming, as if they are about to take a must-pass exam. The spreadsheets for each project are over a hundred pages thick, and yet the team's presentations to the investment committee, while leaving no stone unturned, are concise.

The partner explains that the deal team is attracted to two unusual but compelling ideas. Both are complex; neither are quick wins. Hence the somewhat tortuous session at the investment committee to discuss and critique them. In the end, they will be approved, like many deals that end up consuming a lot of airtime. Bad ideas tend to die a bit faster.

The first idea is to negotiate with pharmaceutical industry giants to carve out unloved parts of their groups that contain older medicines, ex-blockbuster drugs, where a little investment in active marketing of the products would justify *modest* price increases—a few percent per year. The drugs are not monopolies—real competition from low-cost generics exists, but the brand names of these medicines are strong enough to retain a crucial portion of the customer base. Unloved assets sell for weak prices, and so industry giants would accept the price they get from the Firm. The corporate folks running the sales processes at the pharmaceuticals are likely to be more interested in getting a deal done than in optimizing the terms. Their companies are more focused on R&D to find the next clutch of billion-dollar drugs than on tinkering with the pricing and marketing of yesterday's favorites. This dynamic is music to the well-tuned ears of private equity.

And so, by learning from the failed business model of Pharma Corp and refining it enough to make it palatable to buy into—and later sell to someone else at a profit—the team sees terrific opportunity.

The deal team's second idea is to acquire the debt of companies, like Pharma Corp and its peers, that have seen their stock prices crater—whether due to issues specific to the business or because the markets have tainted them for having business plans similar to Pharma Corp's, a kind of guilt by association.

Whether these enterprises turn out to be healthy or need to restructure, their underlying assets have substantial fundamental value, and the keys to this value lie in the loans and bonds of their capital structures. The financial markets have been focused on hedge fund losses in the sector and the forthcoming mooted actions of U.S. lawmakers to oversee the sector more rigorously—these developments have encouraged a "risk-off" mood that has served to dampen valuations. The Firm, if it acts quickly, can acquire the debt at a discount—quietly, while others are preoccupied by the news storm in the wake of Pharma Corp's malaise.

In doing so, as a distressed debt investor, the Firm could control or at least influence the target's fate by being able to accelerate repayment of the paper or by being in a position to drive a debt reorganization, where its best interests are looked after. Interest payments would be received in the meantime, while the target's problems are being worked on.

The idea is not just to buy the distressed debt in the reasonable hope that it might go back up toward par, although if that were to happen, the investment would still be lucrative. It is to utilize the convenient mess in the public eye, quantify the regulatory and political risks, and determine the smarter way to play the situation. What's the smart move here, the Firm asks. What would our key competitors do if they could?

The deal approvals given have a fair degree of flexibility. If the deal team needs to tweak specific terms, they do not need to wait until the following Monday. They can just ask the Founder and the senior-most set of partners for a real-time decision. When the Firm needs to move fast, it can move fast.

Ideally, the investments struck will be signature deals that signal the Firm's arrival in the space. They do not have to write the largest checks, but they do have to be viewed as creative and clever—by its investors as well as by the Firm's rivals. Nobody wants its first deal in a new industry to be met with disbelief at the deal's terms or with skepticism at the chosen strategy. The investments must look like smart bargains that others wish they had the brains and muscle to do themselves.

A couple of closed deals later, and the Firm has a starter portfolio of investments in the pharmaceuticals industry. The money put up might have come from an existing private equity fund or from an investor's pockets directly, wrapped up in a special-purpose vehicle in which the Firm is the exclusive manager of the assets. This is known as warehousing assets. The Firm can use these investments as a springboard to launch a specialized fund as a satellite to the flagships—here, a dedicated fund for life sciences.

The sequence of events I have described was sparked by the masters of private equity seeing creative chances to make money, thinking, *How can I get some of that in a smart way?* And then applying their extreme rigor and relentless execution skills to nail down every detail and not rest until it is done.

This is how it works on the inside. Private equity develops an original investment theme or, as in this case, looks at a series of events and tries to see if there is an opportunity to create value. A small and tight-knit team of investment professionals takes charge of the project and prosecutes it until it is time for their colleagues to critique it and assist in getting to the right answer. The deal check they are responsible for at the major firms in the industry ranges from a few hundred million to over a billion dollars of other people's money. They must know their target company's sectors, financing, management, and competitors. They must know examples of parallel industries that the committee can look to for valuable lessons and harsh questions. And they must keep their contacts fresh and their information current until the exit, many years away. Nothing is plain vanilla about any of it.

And yet cutting a check is only the beginning of a deal, not the end. Until an investment is sold, the money is locked up. The hard work starts as the team tracks the progress of the invested-in business and tracks the thesis that persuaded the investment committee. They do this once a quarter, if not every month—without fail. Course corrections are suggested, missteps are identified, and grenades are dodged.

Crucially, the deal team will evaluate the folks who are running the business—the management. Is anyone not getting the memo, not driving hard or listening to feedback or answering requests for data and insight? Which roles can we upgrade, and how would we do it with the minimum level of disruption, public banter, or, worse, litigation? In essence, the deal team is engaged in a constant process of underwriting and re-underwriting to make sure that everything is under control. It is what would likely happen in the best public companies for the acquisitions they make—but at warp speed and with a fraction of the staff.

This work is called portfolio management, and it's the Noah's Ark that guides a deal from entry to the exit, through discussions at the boardroom level and, more important, between board meetings in working-group sessions with the management team and internally among the deal team. A rough rule of thumb is that a third of the work done on a private equity investment is the entry, a third is portfolio management, and a third is the exit. Each deal will vary, but it's often a good approximation for what happens, and it clarifies that often there is little rest from the starting gun to the finish line. The operating changes to the target, the interventions that private equity demands to change the trajectory of an investment, are about putting the thesis behind a deal into practice. It is this thesis that will form the backbone of the investment's story under private equity ownership.

There is no sugarcoating that selling is the objective from day one. It must be part of the execution plan, the reverse engineering from contemplating what kind of profitable exits are likely to what can be done from the start to make them probable. The mind map of how to sell, and more broadly how to monetize private equity investments, is as complex as it's ever been—one of the options we've not yet covered is selling the investment from one fund managed by the private equity firm, an older-vintage fund, to a newer fund just raised by the same firm. The firm wants to exit the investment and realize a profit, but also wants to hold onto the investment, as it's likely to generate more value in years to come. And so it achieves both objectives by having the older fund sell the investment to the newer fund. In this case, the private equity firm will earn Two and Twenty on both of the funds involved.

Of course, this exit pathway is a creative way to achieve an attractive exit price with a lower risk of the sale falling through, because both funds are managed by the same private equity firm. Two and Twenty is charged on the "new" acquisition, just as if the buying fund had bought a new target, and on the "old" investment being monetized through this exit strategy. Expect to see more of this going forward.

Such moves might raise eyebrows among investors, but if adequately explained—for example, because the target's strategic vision still had many years to implement, significantly beyond the life of the fund, and the next fund is able to carry on the work and look forward to its own exit—then the funds' investors are unlikely to object to the transaction.

The process of private equity investing is exciting and unique. Nowhere else in the business world can relatively young executives have this much influence on established companies and discuss the future of different industries across the global economy with senior management and experts. In this setting, a younger executive can have an impact on enterprises, consumers, the communities touched by the target, the supply chain, and the environment. When you're sitting in offices in Manhattan and Mayfair, how the job works in practice is thrilling and humbling in its raw power to make a huge difference. Once you've done it, few careers can compare in this respect.

And that huge difference extends to making money. The financial rewards in private equity are essential to incentivize the people who make this system work. In the next chapter, we explore this concept further, by turning to the concentration of power in the decision-making bodies and top layers of private equity firms—the elite circles of the industry.

# CHAPTER THREE

# Behind the Curtain

It's David's first day at the Firm. Early December, bright and cold, a year after the financial crisis. The time is 7:30 A.M. David's short walk to his new office from the subway station near the Seagram Building is laced with bracing winds, but they seem to wither at the foot of the most prestigious skyscraper in New York, as if nature does not make the cut past the imaginary velvet rope. The young investment banker has just left Wall Street for Midtown, joining the Firm as an associate, the bottom rung. Just before he crosses the threshold, he looks up to the sky and sees a concave-slope façade of ebony glass and travertine-clad walls stretching well beyond the gray clouds. A brief prayer of gratitude and a wish for good luck, and he steps inside. In his opinion—as well as that of his friends and peers in finance—he's made it to the big leagues. This is it.

The revolving steel doors are huge but somehow look pitiful compared to the width and height of the whole imposing structure. Security is tight. A dozen heavies in dark suits and earpieces roam the lobby, flanked by a dozen more at fixed stations around the rectangular double reception. David runs up a steep but brief flight of steps, one last hurdle before reaching the check-in desk. The new hire spots four others like him, all waiting to be processed and cleared. Five faces, including a woman from Western Europe, three white American men, and a man of Asian descent. That's him.

Fresh out of Wharton, graduating at the top of his class, David ground out two years of invaluable finance experience as a star financial analyst in the mergers and acquisitions group at Goldman Sachs before winning a place at the Firm. He was interviewed for over two months in secret by twenty senior investment professionals who drilled him through countless case studies, financial model exercises, and personality questions. He felt his best answers were when he spoke from the heart, plainly and clearly, because that was when his interviewer would reply with a gentle nod of acknowledgment. Instinctually, he avoided using bland corporatespeak, knowing his prospective bosses would find it distasteful.

Suddenly, in the lobby, David observes as the guards break into smiles. There is commotion as a tall, well-built man in his early fifties, dressed comfortably in a navy flannel suit and thick felt coat, strolls past the theater of the lobby scene, neglecting to remove his custom-made folding Persol sunglasses. He strides into an empty brushed copper elevator lined with red carpet, one of twenty such units carved into two limestone columns in the middle of the hall. A group of six senior Wall Street bankers that had been waiting to use the same elevator parts ways when they see him arrive. The new recruits recognize the man instantly and understand why he was waved through: He is the Founder of the Firm. A visionary, an investment legend, worth three billion dollars and counting.

An hour earlier, just before leaving his one-bedroom apartment in the East Village, the recruit scoured the Firm's website one last time, looking for fresh news that might come up on his first day, even in passing. He recalls his first cursory glances at the site twelve months ago, when he applied, noticing immediately how the Firm looked like it was present everywhere across the world—investing in nearly every industry one could think of, in every major economy and a handful of smaller ones too. He knows that his employer is a phenomenal machine, with thousands of handpicked employees in offices across the key continents. His colleagues invest billions of dollars across sectors and products. They sit at the apex of capitalism, like an ultimate conglomerate, a snapshot of GDP that grows relentlessly. And now, here he is, about to become an insider.

The Firm's website is a slick production, with carefully chosen pictures and words that highlight private equity's contribution to and progress in promoting social causes. Workplace diversity, public engagement, sustainability, community ties, climate resilience, and active citizenship. Awards and recognition for being one of America's "Best Places to Work." Private equity is shown to be about building better businesses, acting as responsible custodians of ordinary workers' money. Ethics, culture, values, and credibility are front and center. When David scanned these photos and phases that morning, what came to his mind was the impression of professional duty, an unimpeachable goal to help investors like the retirees whose pension funds form one of the bedrocks of the investor community. The narrative of the Firm, as told by its web presence, is one that is mission-driven, a mission to serve retirement systems as a for-profit enterprise, in which both retirees and shareholders benefit. The image is curated and manicured, and it is genuine, too.

The org charts displayed on the website exemplify the image of a top blue-chip corporation, with a board of directors that includes non-executive directors drawn from the upper echelons of business and politics, executive leadership groups that span the full suite of corporate functions, and rosters of heavyweight advisors tapped from industry. Experts in government affairs, environmental issues, information technology, public relations, portfolio management, macroeconomic research, legal and compliance, risk management, and other core roles are presented on the same level as the deal professionals. In fact, these full-time "non-deal professionals" can outnumber the deal professionals by two to one. Taken together, the assembly of luminaries looks like the United Nations of finance and business: stately, diverse, and experienced. Layers of committees complete the company sketch—an operating committee here, a management committee there. The roster also gives the appearance of decentralization, with plenty of checks and balances, as one might expect in a multinational enterprise running hundreds of billions of dollars of investors' money.

And yet, already, on his first day, David has the feeling that not everything is quite as it seems. It's all real, it's all genuine, the website is accurate, of course, but there is more to it, more to how the place works in practice—how private equity works behind the scenes. It doesn't feel like it operates like a corporation, even a great one. It feels like a small and tight-knit firm. He has already heard that some employees are more equal than others in certain ways—a fact that has greater implications in private equity than in other fields of asset management. Through the interview process, he has sensed that in private equity firms, decision-making is concentrated. Power is concentrated. And he's understood that perhaps it has to be this way for the results to be as good as they are.

He muses. Maybe this point is more subtle today than it used to be. Certainly, this is what his friends who already work in the private equity industry say. But the fact is, the magnitude of the investment decisions that rest on perhaps a few dozen sets of smart shoulders is immense. As the assets under management grow, the responsibility these individuals have grows too.

There might be two hundred investment professionals in a firm that manages several hundred billion dollars across private capital strategies, with its latest private equity fund sized at, say, twenty billion dollars to invest and with another ten billion dollars left in older funds invested in assets that will need to be sold before too long in order to realize a profit. That's thirty billion dollars of private equity money. David knows that the vital decisions to buy and sell across thirty billion dollars will ultimately fall to a set of, say, twenty deal partners—if that. Thirty billion dollars of investors' money, relying on the judgment of a few handfuls of senior investment professionals.

And so, the new recruit anticipates that to understand how private equity really works, he must understand the people who animate and run the system, such as the folks who run the Firm. David must pay attention to the folks behind the curtain.

David spends the next three hours in bland conference rooms, inhaling facts and policies as part of the employee orientation program. Since the Firm's IPO, this part of the first day has become more formal, filled with serious presentations about regulation, behavior, protocols, rules, expense reports, and other important, if dry, matters. A human resources staffer distributes org charts, and David is astonished at the depth of the teams in oversight and support functions.

David tries to commit it all to memory, but he can't help letting his mind wander to the ornate antique rifles mounted prominently on the walls. He considers how their suggestion of unrestrained, old-fashioned, freewheeling firepower contrasts starkly with the modern organization that he is being briefed on. The analog triggers, the unquestionable purpose, the original chemistry of the gunpowder. Point, shoot, kill. Someone paid a fortune for those guns, or at least they are worth a fortune, and someone wants them to be on display for a reason, he thinks. David is unapologetic about his ambitions; he started with nothing apart from the hardworking principles instilled in him by his working-class family, and he has worked tirelessly since his school days to gain a foothold in this elite world. He vows to do whatever it takes to succeed and to improve his lot.

When David was offered the job, at a total compensation package of $150,000 per year, the head of Human Resources at the Firm was quick to remind him that less than one percent of applicants for an investment professional's role were so lucky. At the time, he mused on an irony of the math: Less than one percent of applicants gained access to the lowest rung of an elite club whose members included the one percent of society by net worth. Despite an inner confidence from knowing he had made the grade to get in, unlike so many of his friends who had applied for similar roles at the major private equity firms, he is daunted by the very powerful people around him.

At 11:00 A.M., orientation ends, and David is immediately staffed on his first project by a partner who—in addition to his day job of doing deals—organizes junior resources on deals. The project is a strategy assignment that will be presented directly to the Founder. Initially, he is puzzled by the assignment. It is not a deal. The work is to update a project with the code name "Endgame." The project is a living creature, refined and improved every six months by several of the partners known to be the

Firm's creative geniuses and contributed to by the other partners who focus on running the Firm and acting as its public figureheads. The goal of the project is to anticipate the optimal ways for the Firm to maximize in scale and profit—identifying market opportunities before they appear to its rivals—and to execute a plan to capitalize on them. The Firm must strike almost in silence to minimize the chance of copycat behavior by competitors. The assignment is so confidential that he is ordered not to discuss it with anyone without permission, even the rest of the incoming class of five associates. David obeys.

The new hire sits in a bullpen with the other recruits, and they are organized in a matrix, as though the rows of busy associates are sophisticated machines in an engine room. The offices wrap around the perimeter of the floor, with the largest ones boasting Central Park views and the smallest without windows at all. The decor is modern and monotone, complete with extensive audiovisual facilities and a huge, fully stocked self-service kitchen that is open all hours, but the furniture is a little worn. Here and there are hints of the urban legend that the Firm acquired the office and all of its furnishings years ago from Enron or one of the other big fallen angels desperate to raise money after a corporate scandal and bankruptcy.

As the legend has it, the Founder personally negotiated to buy everything from the desperate seller at twenty cents on the dollar, from the fifty-year lease to the designer furniture. The seller was facing doom, and its executives were facing jail.

The look and feel of everything is meant to project a firstclass, hardworking, results-driven organization. This goes for the people, too. During the day, everyone looks a bit serious, even when they share a joke or smile, every emotion is a bit measured, and nearly every word spoken is deliberate. Hours can pass without voices being raised; when two colleagues walk down a corridor, the sound of expensive shoes shuffling can be louder than the conversation being held. And then a partner cracks a comment that makes a small cluster of folks laugh, or you might hear the faint sounds of a small "Happy Birthday" singalong or a toast for some other celebration that lasts a few fun minutes. Lavish spreads from Michelin-starred restaurants and famous local delis add a touch of comfort and luxury to every meal in the office. It's all designed to be supportive, to reassure, to reflect the Firm and its status. The employees are well looked after.

David's workspace is generous, with an expensive mechanical worktable that rises and drops to permit typing while standing up. It is built for the very long hours he will soon get used to. The executive he is working under has an office, like other mid-level investment professionals, although it is more of a cubicle with walls than a fancy corner suite. The partner leading the assignment has a proper office, three times larger, like the other nineteen partners of the Firm, showcasing triple floor-to-ceiling light-sensitive glass windows and the very finest views of the world's most expensive stretch of green: Central Park. The assistants sit near their bosses, in clusters, fielding calls and fixing diaries for deals that impact a growing slice of the global economy. Now and then, VIP guests and senior executives pass through the floor and sit down with partners in their offices or in one of the conference rooms. A senator here, a Fortune 500 CEO there; a tech entrepreneur one week, a Hollywood mogul the next. It is the place to be, not just in finance, but probably in all of big business.

The partners mingle freely. They are down-to-earth; they feel at home. After all, they run the place. They are happy to have deal teams stop by for unscheduled chats and questions about work, on tricky parts of investments that need senior guidance.

It's in their interest and part of their nature to be open and relaxed; they have nothing to fear and everything to gain. There is plenty of banter and gossip in the late hours, and for good measure, to break the ice, the partners offer a few delicious snippets now and then. But just because partners mix easily among the troops, it does not mean everyone is equal—this is both fair and understood. The partners don't act or look like rock stars, but it's undeniable they stand apart for who they are, their track record and their choice to keep working as they want to. Many of them could easily have retired, but that would be too boring.

David notices that when partners are around, or appear, some of his colleagues' backs stiffen a little, their voices perk up, their looks get sterner, and their words are more structured. Everyone is more careful, more compact, more positive about making progress. It's not fake, it's just more careful. But David and his fellow new hires all love it, the energy of the place, the sense of purpose and achievement. *There is nowhere better to be,* he and the other young associates repeat each night as they stagger home in taxis to their small apartments, past midnight, exhausted but thinking about work. It's as if they are in Wall Street's answer to the West Wing. There's no comparison, anywhere in finance.

Communication cuts three different ways. Regardless of rank, it is considered best to talk face-to-face. Seven times out of ten, the subject matter is too confidential, too private, too nuanced to be stored in cyberspace forever. Knocking on the office window of a superior and asking for a few minutes signals the importance of the dialog. Nobody does it to waste time. If you can't meet in person, speak on the phone—and keep your comments brief. There is no value added in droning on, and talking without being prepared is the definition of wasting time. And last, send an email if you really must, but never write anything negative.

The scariest email David sees in his first week is internal, short, from one of his bosses; it reads simply, "Let's chat."

Aside from internal messenger applications, typically used to keep the flow of work efficient within bullpens and across teams that need to liaise with each other, this is how folks communicate, and it's also how they measure the pros and cons of each method of communication. When billions of dollars are at stake on a deal, how a point is made—and heard—counts.

Responsibility is handed down at the earliest opportunity, and the workflow relies on delegating to those who can step up. With his work priorities clear, David is left to his own devices, the internal messenger platform and frequent check-ins with his senior colleagues serving as handy progress guides. And the workload is so demanding, the deadlines so tight, that there is little time to waste and nowhere to hide if someone does. You have either produced the output requested of you, or you have not. There is no try. With this clear and extreme workday pattern, stretching long into the midnight hours, there is no need to be watched by the CCTV system that sits visibly overhead. You end up being your own toughest taskmaster.

The three members of David's project team meet every morning and evening to review progress and set tasks. He is encouraged to be inquisitive, to play Devil's advocate, to probe, and to argue. It is immensely refreshing. The partner explains that the work is much more than a business plan review or strategic update. Since the Firm's IPO, the Founder and the partners have realized that the listed market seems to value more highly the stable, recurring management fees that the Firm brings in, come rain or shine—the two percent—over the larger, supposedly more volatile performance fees that crystallize when investment gains are monetized—the twenty percent. The stock price is largely driven by a regular stream of management fees under long-term contracts, and as assets under management grow for the Firm, the stock's attractiveness to public market investors increases because this fee pile grows alongside the assets. Of course, there is a strong track record of delivering performance fees on top, because the funds perform well, but these are incremental to the equity story; they do not underpin it. For the stock market, the Two is mission-critical. The Twenty is important, but it is not taken for granted.

Put bluntly, the fate of the Firm's stock price rests just as much on the growth of its assets under management as on how well those assets perform. The funds must continue to outperform their benchmarks handsomely, but they do not have to shoot the lights out even further than they already do, and certainly there is no extra return in taking outsize risks to make the fund returns stellar in every single vintage.

And although the Firm's head count is growing, especially now that the Firm is a public company with all the middle and back office functionality that goes with that, head count is not growing as quickly as the assets under management are growing. This means the Firm profits from a rising pile of management fees paid by a rising pile of assets under management. That provides the Firm with operating leverage.

The largest players in the private equity industry have all come to the same realization. What is different about the Firm is the way it plans to take advantage of the phenomenon. Sure, it will do what the others are doing: develop new fund strategies across sectors, geographies, and products as a robust growth engine for raising funds. These initiatives will steadily increase inflows from investors. It will continue to be responsible and ensure that performance for investors does not dip. But this is routine fare. The

Firm is determined to differentiate itself by moving the needle off the charts, from managing a couple hundred billion dollars to managing close to a trillion within the next decade, and more beyond that. David has the heady task of compiling data across the Firm on how this master plan is going and analyzing the financial impact on the Firm's current trajectory.

There are two parts to Endgame, David's assigned project. Both strategies aim to increase the Firm's penetration of the total amount of money available to invest from pension funds, sovereign wealth funds, insurance companies, and high-net-worth families—and ultimately from mom-and-pop investors too, who can't currently invest in the Firm's funds directly. The Firm estimates that the potential pool of this cash is tens of trillions of untapped dollars.

The first part of the project team's strategy is developing platforms that do not offer a natural or preset moment when investors' money is to be withdrawn or redeemed. In other words, the investors are essentially locked in. A traditional private equity fund is forced to wind up after, say, ten years, at which point it must return all the money to its investors that hasn't already been paid out to them, including deal profits (net of fees). A credit fund is often structured along similar lines, or it may have another fixed-term arrangement with its investors. This loop sets up a predictable cycle, where new funds start to be raised when existing funds approach the end of their lifetime. Investors then have an opportunity to decide whether they want to reinvest in the same strategy or put their money elsewhere, either with the same firm or a rival or not at all. There is a clear way out, and the process is transparent and well understood by investors.

From the perspective of a private equity firm, however, the

hard break with investors' money after the fixed term of a private equity fund creates uncertainty. Will existing investors reinvest the same amount of money? Will they reinvest more or less money? Will new investors commit money? Even if the fund-raising process is likely to succeed, as it would be for a successful franchise with a long track record of strong performance, nothing is guaranteed. A rival could emerge and divert funds to its more compelling proposition. An ethics or regulatory issue or other grenade could sap the firm's appeal, precisely at the moment when it most wants investors to make easy decisions to recommit money. And if the firm's stock is listed on a public exchange, the market might not give full credit to the share price for its private equity franchise, because of the uncertainty associated with the fundraising process for funds with a fixed life—even if the fund's terms allow for extensions of that life by, say, a few years.

In contrast, a new vehicle that brings in cash on the explicit basis that it may be invested in perpetuity could "structure away" this issue, and the associated management fees would be payable for as long as the firm and the investor are in business. And, of course, there would be performance-related fees on top, too. There will be some variation of Two and Twenty still payable— but with investors' money locked up under management by the firm. These investment platforms are known as "permanent capital" or "perpetual capital" and they are often publicly listed.

In the Firm's case, David must amass ideas from across the Firm on the scope and profitability of the market opportunity for such vehicles. At present, perpetual capital vehicles represent less than ten percent of the Firm's assets under management. David's superiors tell him that the objective is to reach over fifty percent within ten years.

The idea is to cement a stable, long-duration stream of fee

revenue for the Firm and help both the Firm and its investors save time on the cumbersome hassle of a fund renewal process every few years. It is the holy grail for the Firm, because the money handed over to it to manage does not have a limited life. Like a ship moving from a narrow channel into open waters, this new strategy opens up vast opportunities for the Firm to grow its investment franchise even faster than it was doing before.

As he absorbs what he is hearing, David muses that just this morning he was taught that fundraising is part of the lifeblood of a private equity firm—and yet here he is working on a secret plan for a version of . . . immortality. Management fees without the ticking clock of a finite fund life, helping to drive the Firm's stock price higher as the Firm's profits increase year after year. The concept is not new; it is inspired by Berkshire Hathaway, the listed investment vehicle led by Warren Buffett. But the application to private equity firms is novel, and at this stage, none of the Firm's rivals are focused on it.

David collects and synthesizes fifteen permanent capital fund plans from across the Firm, including from the private equity, real estate, insurance, credit, and infrastructure investing teams. Sticky pots of other people's money—with perpetual fees. If the plans are followed, the Firm's assets under management will grow by at least twenty billion dollars within the decade.

The second component of the project team's strategy is the mission to get the masses to invest in private equity funds and other private capital investment vehicles. At present, ordinary retail investors like members of the general public cannot invest in private capital funds under decades-old SEC regulations designed to protect such non-experts from complex products they might not fully understand. In other words, mom and pop are pretty much off-limits as direct investors for private capital.

But Americans and citizens in many other developed markets are woefully short of retirement savings, and the Firm believes that its funds can be presented as a solution for this chronic underfunding by providing superior returns, at acceptable risk, to grow investors' savings through 401(k) or other retirement plans. Private equity and similar funds can help bridge the gap over the long term by generating the savings required for a comfortable retirement. The Firm's mission is to tap into the tens of trillions of dollars of retail money that might be up for grabs—if only the law would allow it—without regulation that might make it too burdensome to go down this road.

Protecting ordinary workers' monthly savings is of paramount concern. And so, David is tasked with amalgamating ideas from across the Firm, and its government lobbying and regulatory advisors, on how complicated funds for sophisticated investors such as sovereign wealth funds could be adapted to a retail audience. Perhaps the funds could be regulated more tightly, but not restrictively in a way that would impede the work of the investment professionals. Perhaps mom and pop could benefit from due diligence conducted by richer investors and somehow rely on it for their own purposes. Perhaps retail-friendly funds could target lower-risk, lower-return investments to make only what they need for retirement and no more. The idea is to fix in the psyche of ordinary citizens a mentality to see investing in private equity in the same routine way as investing in the stock market via a Vanguard or BlackRock mutual fund, index fund, or ETF. Those well-known investment firms manage trillions of dollars of retail money.

David's thoughts wander to his parents. Would he want their 401(k) invested in the Firm's stock or the Firm's funds? Or both? What would investing in private equity—and its close cousins across the product range in private capital—mean for them? Would it help them achieve their retirement objectives? The words on the pages: retail investors. He sees faces instead of letters, life goals instead of numbers. He sees his parents, his uncles and aunts, his teachers at school and the local doctors and nurses he knows from his home community. He wonders if they would ever understand what they are invested in, especially if it goes wrong. For a moment, he worries if they would think he is doing something wrong, even though he is not. In fact, the work he is doing on retail investors is likely one of the best opportunities that his parents' money should look at. But would they believe it? And could he guarantee it would work out well? He asks himself whether the industry is too opaque to be properly appreciated.

As his work impulses take over, David snaps to attention—and his thoughts return to the task at hand: determining what these initiatives mean in terms of the Firm's economics. The objective is to scale up to the size of a firm like BlackRock, but keep Two and Twenty at the core of the fee model where possible. He realizes that both of the initiatives he is working on, if successful, would help drive up the Firm's stock price to new heights.

David's project balances a tough set of delicate considerations. What is best for investors? For the Firm to diversify and expand, as is being explored? What is best for the Firm? Are the goals aligned? He does not raise these questions with his deal team, because the nuances do not manifest explicitly. These are subtle points, and likely to be controversial if misinterpreted.

The young associate hands his efforts over to his superior, a mid-level professional with the title "Principal," who augments the action plans for the next steps. This principal highlights a key point that serves as a decisive reason to proceed at pace: The data suggests that the Firm's relationships with existing investors are so strong, based on a track record of solid investment performance, that fundraising efforts for these two initiatives are likely to meet with quick success. Sovereign wealth funds—for example, some of those set up in the Middle East and Asia—have the kind of ultra-long investment horizons that permanent capital vehicles can be readily marketed to. The systems of government in these regions often involve ruling families or dominant political parties, and for this reason they have planning horizons far longer than the governments of Western countries, with elected leaders who serve for fixed terms.

The Firm can start there, before American pension funds see the bandwagon moving and consider whether to join in. Retail investors do genuinely need healthier retirement savings, and legislators and regulators have started to consult on the art of the possible when considering how private equity funds could cater to retail investors. They have started to analyze rolling back existing protections—also known as red tape.

It is then the partner's turn to add his lens. The partner overseeing the deal team, a natural diplomat, tones down the language on economics, leaving more for live discussion and less on the page. He cannot stand the idea of gloating about the economics. The numbers that underpin Endgame are so compelling that they do not need to be highlighted, and so he carefully rebalances the language in the deal team's materials for the investment committee. He is also exceptionally well connected in the industry and drafts pages himself to set the opportunity against what he knows is going on at his rivals' shops—anything that could steal the Firm's thunder on these plans. By framing the picture against the backdrop of competitors' activities, he imparts a sense of urgency to the discussion that is more subtle than shouting loudly about how much money can be made and what these initiatives could do for the Firm's stock. The partner acts like a polished statesman.

David is humbled by the power of what they are all working on and how fully each member of the deal team is briefed. The assignment is more important to the Firm than any one private equity deal or piece of credit business. David is also impressed; as the project has moved up through the deal team, the story has gotten sharper and the messages clearer, and yet they are more gently delivered. And the night before the presentation to the Founder, when he asks his colleagues whether it's better for investors to put their money in the Firm's funds or the Firm's stock, he is met with his bosses' knowing expressions. The answer is obvious: "Both."

Investors are best served by putting some of their cash in the Firm's funds to generate much-needed returns, the partner on the deal team explains, and by putting some of the rest of their cash in the Firm's stock to benefit from the profitable and fast growth of the Firm and the frequently paid distributions. The point of Endgame is to get a share of both types of wallet. A win-win. All of the workstreams detailed in the project, if you cut through the detail, lead back to this result. All roads lead to Rome.

As he thinks about the economics, David recalls the water cooler talk among his peers during the induction program about how much money they could make if they were to progress through the hierarchy to the top. A senior partner can be worth a hundred million dollars in their forties. Some are worth much more. Deep down—or perhaps not so deep down—the associates admit to themselves that this is a big part of why clever and ambitious men and women walk through those revolving steel doors downstairs every morning. They are eager to achieve life-changing money and power.

The top folks have done it.

They don't wait to enter the skyscraper.

The top folks could own the skyscraper if they wanted to.

They embody the influence and presence of the industry they lead.

A handful of the most senior partners, those who have the strongest investment track records and perform management roles on top of their investing duties—and are among the largest individual shareholders—are the ones who count the most to investors. They are the handful deemed to be "key employees" in the Firm's fund documents, individuals without whom the business may not be able to function at all. In fact, such an eventuality would constitute one of the narrow circumstances in which investors could set in train a motion to get their money out ahead of schedule. They are called "key employees" for a reason, despite the strong bench of talent who work alongside them. What is striking is that they are not what you or I would call employees in the traditional sense of the word. They have employment contracts of sorts, but they are far more like owners than employees. This is why their interests are closely aligned with the financial health and future of the Firm.

Stepping back from this sketch, we can make a few points about the workings of the industry. Private equity is not a democracy, and it is not run by groupthink. Deal teams listen to each other, collaborate freely, and have autonomy over many aspects of their work. The same is true at multiple pairings of

individuals across the resource pyramid—from colleagues sparring over clashing ideas or conflicting data to engaged discourse
on how portfolio companies are performing. But power is not
evenly or thinly spread. What the Firm's Founder and partners
aim for is what drives the direction and speed of travel for investors.

The significance of this power concentration in private equity
is undeniable. Not only is immense wealth accumulated in the
hands of the few, but these individuals also have profound influence on increasingly broad swaths of the economy. One important ramification of this is the control or material influence of a
tiny number of private individuals over hundreds of thousands of
employees and their communities, with far more power than, say,
Wall Street banks. More power and more consequence, because
in the case of private equity what is certain is that the businesses
involved are there to be traded—to be bought and sold—on a
regular basis like financial assets. And ideally, when these assets
are sold, they are left in much better shape than when they were
bought—not just financially but from a social point of view too,
as measured by their impact on the communities they serve,
on the economy, and on society in general. The value creation
through private equity ownership should be impactful at many
levels.

In turn, this means that the social considerations involved
with any business invested in or lent to by private equity (or
private capital in general) are balanced—often more than
balanced—with the constant imperatives to make money for
the investors and the firm. The private equity folks who control
these decisions are not elected representatives, and in most cases,
they are keen to stay out of the spotlight. Most of the employees

in portfolio companies and the citizens in the communities they impact might not meet these individuals, even if they meet the management of the portfolio companies. We must look at this reality with our eyes open.

Consider what this implies for our reliance on private equity. When we look at it through the prism of how fragile the economy can at times become, it's clear that the top folks in private equity are increasingly important to our collective fortunes. We rely on them not only to help keep our retirement systems and college endowments on track but also to steward increasingly large portions of the economy. They are tasked with making sound decisions when they buy and sell and finance targets, not only for investors and themselves but also for the communities they shape with the decisions they make. That is why ethics, real transparency, and judgment must be at the heart of where money is allocated from investors to private equity firms. Performance alone is not enough—not going forward.

That is also why the media spotlight that is increasingly focused on senior figures in private equity has some justification. Arguably, these investment folks are as important as other business and thought leaders we already think of in the conversation around the impact on our economy—and society—whether we are talking about the CEOs of the Big Tech companies or the Wall Street banks. What they stand for and what motivates them is part and parcel of the jobs they do. They are not only the "key employees" in fund documents between their investors and their firm—they are also key people in our economy.

And for aspiring hires like David who want to reach the heights where the Founder and the senior partners sit, the demands of private equity form the crucible that will determine if they make it. The job requires a particular mindset that explains how and why—on the individual, micro level—private equity has attained such macro dominance. It is this core DNA within private equity professionals, how to identify it and hone it, to which we turn in the chapters ahead.

# CHAPTER FOUR

# We Eat Our Own Cooking

"Sounds like a problem. Tk."

The nightmare starts when I wake up: a forwarded email from the Founder at 6:21 A.M. Just two curt sentences, twenty letters, ending with his usual shorthand for "thank you." The message was brief, but it was loaded. The Founder, I realize, has read and absorbed the contents of an explosive fifty-page update memo from one of the private equity deal teams, including three thick supporting decks of legal and restructuring analysis from counsel, plus the financial model. My throat sticks as I scroll down. The materials were sent to him six hours ago. The situation is grave.

The Founder's message is like Morse code, and by now I am fluent in it: *There's an issue with this investment. It's bad, and it could be terminal. Handle this in parallel with your day job. It's not just the deal team's problem, it's all our problem. Update me, explain the numbers at stake and what we are going to do about it. It's your job to explain what the rescue looks like and its chance of success. If and only if failure is inevitable, figure out how to limit the pain. Investigate and report to me directly.* The Founder will expect a crisp update within a few hours—with concrete progress.

I am not any better an investor than the partner in charge of the deal, but I am fresh blood. An additional perspective and

voice, hopefully accretive. A cold read of the mess. The investment is falling headfirst into a chasm of total capital loss, and
before events spiral irretrievably out of control, I am being
ordered to fix what can be fixed. The deal team is exhausted,
fueled now by fear rather than greed, and they require reinforce-
ments at the senior level. I don't care that I was not offered a
choice to work on this matter, as the Founder well knows. In
truth, I desperately want to turn the investment around. I have
the same share of profit or loss in the deal as the partner in
charge—and I have plans for the profit we told ourselves was
going to come. I want us to win.

By 11:30 A.M., I have been debriefed by the deal team and our
Wall Street investment banking advisors. In response, I offer a
dispassionate critique of their analysis and rework the action
plan. I do not replace the deal team's lead partner, and there is
no hint of a bruised ego or defensiveness from him; our collective economics are too important to waste precious time on
such games. Our task is to work together, and we desperately
hope to devise a solution to what is plainly shaping up to be a
catastrophic failure.

The Firm has invested four hundred million dollars in the
leveraged buyout of Plastix Corp, a specialty producer of high-
grade chemicals used in the manufacture of aircraft, motor vehicles, and industrial components. The company's products make
possible the plastics used to make airplane and car frames lighter
as well as the delicate parts of laptops that get smaller with each
new model. Such plastics require performance materials that
are highly resistant to heat, friction, and other forms of physical
stress. A kind of nonstick surface but far more advanced.

Plastix is a pioneer in this field, with a rich history. The company was founded after World War II by a Nordic Nobel laure-

ate in chemistry and remained in his family's hands until the grandchildren sold in the mid-2000s to a Russian-American billionaire at a price fit for a trophy asset. His objective was to grow Plastix's market share in attractive verticals such as electric transport and to make complementary acquisitions. Unfortunately, these dreams were interrupted when the financial crisis hit other parts of his empire, including a large and foolish derivative position on the U.S. mortgage market in which he had bet against the finest traders on Wall Street and lost. He was subsequently forced into a humiliating bankruptcy, and he ended up losing key assets. The tycoon's lending banks in New York, having been awarded control of Plastix as the crown jewel of his remaining holdings, hired advisors to auction it. They had no interest in running the business; their sole mission was to recover their loans at a modest rate of interest and generate some transaction fees from the sale. A low reserve price was set, and Plastix was put on the block.

Bids came in from all over the world, including submissions from private equity firms and strategic acquirers, many of which came to the table with long lists of conditions. But the banks weren't interested in bids that came with the ability to back out if the financing markets—or Plastix's prospects—deteriorated, an ability that gets committed in "material adverse change" clauses. The banks wanted their loans back, and they didn't want to wait months for that to happen. A lower bid, but one free of onerous conditions, was accepted instead. It wasn't a fire sale price, but it felt like a smart bargain. The Firm won, and the deal closed within twelve weeks.

The partner leading the deal was confident of making three to four times the money he was responsible for on behalf of the Firm's investors. Hot on the heels of a home run in a similar sector, the buyout of a specialty metals producer, the partner had thought he was on a roll. His game plan: Buy the business somewhat on the cheap from desperate lending banks; cut out the fat by negotiating hard with trade unions and suppliers; update the plants to focus on the most profitable products; and then wait for the first bullish window of opportunity to flip it to an Asian conglomerate who had lost out in the auction by being too cautious on the price and conditionality of its bid. It had worked well last time, with the specialty metals producer, so why not double up? The financial analysis was supportive; the data was sound.

Twelve weeks later, however, the investment has soured irretrievably. The team has gone too hard and too fast in slashing headcount, and the plants are crippled by rolling strikes protesting the new owner's lack of due consultation with workers and overly harsh severance terms for the departing employees. Despite upgrading management to better-qualified executives, the company was not able to adapt adequately to disruption in its production facilities; meanwhile, major customer orders have been delayed at short notice or have gone unfulfilled. With the business paralyzed, clients have started to look to healthier competitors.

Another twelve weeks later, Plastix's order book of forward revenues is looking morbidly thin. The investment was leveraged, as buyouts almost always are, with each investor's dollar matched by two dollars from bondholders. And despite the Firm's considerable expertise in negotiating bond terms and navigating problems, Plastix feels like it is living on borrowed time.

The high fixed cost of running Plastix's huge chemical plants in Europe and in the Rust Belt means working capital is quickly becoming a perilous issue, and existing lines of liquidity from its banks are nearly exhausted. Plastix needs an immediate cash infusion to survive its self-inflicted wounds. And this is why the Founder had received the pack of materials that led him to involve me. In short, the materials had a clear and urgent request: Inject fifty million dollars in the next week, and another fifty million dollars in the coming quarter, or face losing the investment. This vote of confidence will calm the unions, the customers, and the employees; by thus lowering the temperature, the deal team can create the space to reorient the restructuring plans and win back clients. In the context of a long-term investment, around five years in the making, the current moment of impending potential doom may yet be reduced to a terrible but one-time blip.

In order to make any kind of move, whether in the form of the requested cash infusion or otherwise, we first have to look the deal in the mirror and report back to the Founder exactly what we see. We look squarely at the blemishes and scars on the investment and ask honestly what, if anything, still looks good enough to salvage. Whether we are better off walking away.

We then need to repeat this punishing exercise of reflection and investment revalidation in an emergency session with the investment committee. In practical terms, we are being asked to re-underwrite the investment—and we know that asking for an extra hundred million dollars to invest will be harder than securing approval for the first four hundred million dollars. We have to put as much effort into investigating and prosecuting the right thing to do on this rescue as we would on a shiny new billion-dollar investment—perhaps more, or at least in an atmosphere of justified skepticism at the investment committee. The goal of our new assignment is not to make a *return on* our investors' capital. It is to first make a *return of* our investors' capital.

To avoid a write-off, a zero, pretty much at any reasonable cost. That is what the Firm is focusing on the most. And it is as much about not wanting to lose money as it is about wanting to turn a profit on the investment at some point in the future.

Before we see what happened next for the troubled Plastix deal, which is inspired by real events, let's take a moment and unpack the underlying private equity mindset at play here.

Let's start with a major differentiator between a master of private equity and other good finance professionals on Wall Street. A private equity employee is not a salaried employee in the same way a good banker is when advising on mergers and acquisitions, especially if they are an investment professional. They have a personal incentive for their work to succeed, in the form of equity participation in the outcome of the deal, not just a cash and stock bonus if the deal completes. Their incentive largely comes in the result, years after the deal has been announced. As a result, there is an ingrained sense of personal ownership in private equity that does not exist in a comparable form elsewhere on Wall Street. When masters of private equity buy into a company or lend to it as a creditor, they will think and act—on a personal basis—as if they are actually the owner of the business. They are proactive in assuming individual as well as group responsibility for a deal and work hand in glove with the management team of that business to create value. It's like the deal they have sunk investors' money into is not only the center of their demanding job; it's an important part of their life. And yet compared to the raw emotion of ownership that an entrepreneur or family-held company might have, this feeling of ownership is more nuanced. A master of private equity should also, unlike a traditional business owner, have the ability to detach to analyze problems—and when to sell out—when required.

Why do they walk this tightrope? Their compass is their true interest in the deal. It is not the ego; it is the profit that can be made for investors and for their firms. With this filter permanently switched on, their eyes are fixed on the economics—because the investment is a long-term transaction. A trade, for gain, but with an operating business and not a mere financial instrument. The equity or credit invested is not a strategic investment over a long horizon, like Amazon or Apple or Google or Microsoft might make over decades. It's more like a temporary investment that they are paid quite handsomely to make a high return on within just a few years.

Yes, they want the deal's journey to incorporate a learning curve for employees, they want the broader community fabric to benefit, and they want the products or services generated for clients to improve. But in the end, the point is to exit, and they will not hesitate to do just that. A seasoned investor is not interested in congratulations when money goes in; they prefer recognition—and their slice of spoils—when even more money comes out.

And so, what drives the iron grip of the owner mentality in private equity is the imperative to make the deal work, starting with the iron law of never losing the investors' money. By exercising their control or significant influence over portfolio companies, the investment professionals effectively live and breathe these businesses, pulling levers to protect the money invested and to ensure that it grows.

This delicate balance of taking personal ownership on the one hand and being dispassionate on the other hand manifests most vividly when private equity is playing defense. When a deal is going wrong, private equity bares its teeth. The range of responses to a crisis will vary among firms, but in the case of a leveraged buyout like Plastix, most deal teams will consider negotiating a grace period with the company's debtholders to make room for the investment to work through its problems. They will look to reduce costs, even if the necessary rightsizing measures are likely to be painful for the business. Capital expenditure beyond essential maintenance may well be postponed to when the investment is in better shape. There will be a resolve to administer the medicine required, even if the patient finds it to be bitter. This is simply part of being objective and keeping one's eye on the prize of a lucrative exit.

The savviest, most aggressive firms with expertise in distressed situations will not hesitate to engage in dogfights with creditors, suppliers, or anyone else daring to claim a share of their asset— if needed. And it is partly because of this implicit threat of conflict that counterparties like bond investors, when sitting on the other side of the boardroom table from private equity investment professionals to discuss a problem on an investment that is leveraged, as with Plastix, are likely to listen and be accommodative to try resolving the problem first, before it is inevitable that the parties clash.

The interests of investors in private equity funds are aligned with their private equity managers because both sides are keenly awaiting their returns. Retirement systems want to pay out pension checks for their teachers, firefighters, and healthcare workers. Private equity firms want to pay themselves carried interest, their cut of profits. It would be nonsensical to walk away from a struggling deal when there's a chance of a turnaround. Investment professionals tend to stick with a deal through its lifetime, whether it is a winner or ends up being a loser.

The reality of being chained to a frustrating investment for years is partly why discussions in the investment committee about putting money to work in the first place are so rigorous and frank. Twentysomething associates are empowered to question the model's assumptions, and as the pyramid narrows on the way up, the economics at stake increase significantly, and the scrutiny intensifies accordingly. They're all asking each other this question: What if we have to live with this deal for years, only to recover only what we invested—or worse. How likely is it that we lose money? When an investment is discussed in portfolio reviews, the group will be thinking along similar lines: Where is this deal going? Are we expecting a monetization soon, perhaps through a dividend or asset sale or a full exit? Or is this likely to stagnate or even go backward?

The bottom line: In private equity, you are not an advisor. You are a principal. A new recruit in private equity must accept this reality because the job isn't like investment banking or management consulting. You eat what you cook. The hardest work often happens after you have closed a deal. This kind of discipline, to accept that you must stick with investments without an easy option to separate, can act as a clear litmus test for commitment and determination for an investment professional. It's one thing to postpone a planned vacation for a big new deal; it's quite another to make repeated personal sacrifices—potentially for years—because a poor investment needs more attention. And, of course, the intensity of the work is more stressful when things are going wrong. If you're part of a team of three or four investment professionals and you've invested hundreds of millions of other people's dollars, you feel to a tangible extent the weight of responsibility not to lose it.

To see how this attitude of responsibility plays out on a day-to-day basis, let's return to the Plastix sketch. Ironically, it was an excess of zeal to do well—human error under self-generated pressure to repeat or exceed the success of a past investment—that led the deal team close to disaster. They were impatient to make good on the billion dollars of profit that their financial models showed was possible, and their execution on Plastix went awry. We rejoin the deal team as they prepare to salvage the investment for the investors, and for themselves. They are preparing for war.

"If we follow our money, we'll make a double. Eventually."

My opening words to the investment committee are blunt. We can either put more money into the business and make a respectable return, or we can refuse to back the company, knowing that the outcome will almost certainly be failure. There is no point regretting the lost chance to make our investors several times their money within four years, as we originally projected was possible. We cannot change history. We can now expect to make only twice the total amount of money invested, and we now expect it to take longer, I explain to the committee, perhaps as long as eight years. This extended horizon is needed to allow for correcting missteps and getting back on track with improving the operations. But at least the deal will be a success—for our investors and for us. Making twenty percent out of a profitable deal is better than making nothing. A failure has zero profit to share.

We review the fundamental attributes of the investment. The company has a strong franchise, with high and stable market share and leading chemical products. Opportunities to grow

include executing bolt-on acquisitions and investing in compelling new niches with high-growth potential, such as recycled
and biodegradable products. Despite the reductions in headcount, deeper layers of fat are still waiting to be cut. We have
upgraded the management team and retained the technical
bench of talent, all of whom have a hefty share of their modest
net worth at stake on the deal and are locked into compensation
plans that only pay out when we exit profitably. Management
is aligned. The acute issue is short-term liquidity, not a chronic
problem with the business. Our judgment about the longer-term
prospects of this company remains correct.

Not everyone buys this story. In the investment committee,
several partners play the role of our opposition, with one peer
acting less as the Devil's advocate than his appointed execu-
tioner. Their lines are well rehearsed, but the skepticism is both
understandable and entirely in our investors' best interests. *How
will throwing more money be the solution to this problem? Why are
we sure that we are not investing good money after bad? What are
the differences between our initial beliefs about this project and our
beliefs now?* And so on. The grilling lasts for nearly three hours.
In the end, we review what has gone wrong with the company,
assign responsibility for fixing the mistakes, and agree on next
steps.

To relieve the cash crunch, we propose that the Firm's funds
will be lent to the company via a new debt facility, senior in security to the existing debt that we raised in the financing markets
for the leveraged buyout. Fortunately, the debt used to finance
the buyout was negotiated overwhelmingly in the Firm's favor,
with Wall Street banks eager to please, and so it will be straightforward to obtain the creditors' approval for our new "rescue"
facility. We will advance the monies on what is known as a "super

senior" basis, meaning that our new money will be at the front of the line of creditors to be repaid by the company, and the interest on this new debt facility will be paid first.

In other words, we will make the business promise to prioritize, over all others, the principal and interest payable to us. We control the board of directors, so making this promise will be easier than if we did not have representation on the board. The existing debt is held by insurance companies and index fund–style credit funds—passive folks we are used to dealing with efficiently. They can't take over the business and run it, nor do they want to. They will have to accept more risk. And the interest rate on our new money will be higher than usual for the most senior debt in the capital structure, as a reward for the hard work we are about to do and the risk we are taking by following our investors' money with more of their money in order to put this investment right.

This solution is fair, we reason, because we are the ones prepared to commit more capital when the company finds itself in a crisis. We are the ones taking the lead, and that lead entails fresh risks for our investors and for us—not least our reputation for making sound investments. Risks that, in truth, we had a hand in creating, but then again, the company was not in a good position under its prior owners, either. It had a complex history and it was for sale. We had good intentions in our actions, even though we made mistakes. The management we hired agrees that in this urgent situation this is the right course of action. Plastix has the option of shopping our proposal to the market, but that process would take time and there is no guarantee that more compelling terms could be finalized in time. On the other hand, we are ready, and we can invest immediately.

The next steps are for Plastix to take the capital infusion in two shots, a little like a vaccine, with the first or prime shot taken within a few days of our investment committee's approval, and the second or booster shot to be delivered within ten weeks. With a bit of luck and the addition of liquidity, the business might achieve some immunity from its cash-starved malaise, and we might kickstart it into sharp recovery.

The irony was, we do not trust ourselves to be right. Our weapon of choice, investing in the company via debt rather than equity, is a backup plan in case the investment is doomed but we just cannot see it. We consider, and structure for, the possibility that we are wrong a second time. Clear as crystal in the credit documentation for the facility is a package of protections, called covenants, that gives us extra power over the company—especially if the situation deteriorates.

If the business does not respond to the actions that we proposed and goes bankrupt, we can invoke these covenants in order to keep control of Plastix. Whether the company experiences more strikes by the workforce or loses more key clients or is hurt in any other material way, we are able to fight our corner if Plastix ends up on the ropes. The covenants allow us to accelerate a mandatory repayment of the new debt facility, potentially triggering a controlled restructuring in order for the business to start over, with us in the driver's seat as the most senior lender. If the company's downfall results in the price of the buyout debt falling to distressed levels, we can buy it ourselves in order to have more say at the negotiating table during a restructuring. We are fully prepared to go on the attack, and are trying to keep our options open to do so.

If our investors had been a fly on the wall during the investment committee's deliberations over Plastix, they would have been proud of us in our capacity as fierce custodians of their money. We are prepared to do whatever it takes to protect their downside, and we are not running away from the mess. We have a contingency in place to keep hold of the asset in case our rescue fails. Why? It is our fiduciary duty to try until there is no hope left. And also because if our investors make money, then we make money. We're aligned.

The deal team's lead partner, eager to redeem himself, is obsessed with making right the original errors made on the investment. During the investment committee meeting, he takes personal responsibility for each lapse of judgment. He knows that he and the rest of the deal team had been overly eager to force through changes at Plastix rather than managing them more prudently. There is no corporatespeak, no attempt at a cover-up, no finger-pointing. He raises his hand and owns up to his mistakes. He weaves through reviewing parallel workstreams on the project with fluidity and frankness, from cost savings to acquisition targets to incentives for clients to switch back to the company's products. He recounts that he has apologized directly to the unions, in a way they are not used to hearing from executives, and his humility has stopped the bleeding at the plants, with the strikes called off. At the end of the investment committee discussion, when the Founder has the final say and approves our proposals, it is partly because we have made ourselves accountable. He recognizes the raw hunger to win.

However, there is no free pass for mishandling the deal in the first place. The lead partner is given a rough message. He keeps his profit share in the deal as an incentive to rectify the situation but is also warned that if the medicine we prescribe to Plastix doesn't work, his economics in the rest of the private equity fund will be reduced. His track record already includes one troubled asset still owned by the Firm with zero profit paid out after nine years, and although it is fair to survive one mistake, he will not survive two. It is time for him to bring something to the table.

There is another thorny issue. We are mindful of the unspoken fact that links the headache of this deal to the fastest-growing part of the Firm—the credit funds, which are set to grow into the largest of the private capital investment strategies in years to come. With interest rates set by central banks at very low levels, the credit funds' proven and consistent ability to generate yield is of enormous interest to the Firm's investors, many of whom invest across multiple investment strategies for private capital managed by the Firm—from credit to private equity, for example.

Part of the credit funds' business involves trading with the same type of debt investors—and often the very same firms—as those that hold Plastix's buyout debt. If the Firm is too aggressive with them in its attempt to rescue this one deal, no matter how much sense that might make for the investors in the private equity fund that owns Plastix, it could put at risk these important relationships that serve and nourish the credit funds' business. It's a headache that everyone at the Firm wishes they didn't have to deal with. The lead partner is aware of this, of course, and the reality that if the next steps are not handled carefully, there could be collateral damage to the credit business.

We do not have the freedom to prioritize one part of the Firm over another, to set a troubled private equity investment's prospects against the interests of the credit franchise. We know that as partners it is our job to help make both sets of economics work if we can. Whereas in the past we might have been far more aggressive with debt investors in buyouts that proved to be challenging, today there is more than one deal at stake.

Taken together, the core aspects of taking responsibility—from living an investment through a good or poor result to managing contrasting interests across separate private capital funds to working to rectify a spoiled deal—reveal a crucial aspect of the identity needed to thrive as a master of private equity.

The next chapter concerns another core aspect of the private equity mindset when making investments: attraction to complexity. Identifying it, quantifying the risks, and gauging the return from resolving it. We will investigate how to use complexity as a source of value when making investments and how complexity can fuel profit for private equity.

# CHAPTER FIVE

# Running into a Burning Building

Chaos can be profit in disguise.

This belief is core for the masters of private equity. They love a mess to analyze, some disruption to decipher, or an economic firefight to bring to heel. When hunting for fresh deals, they actively seek out dislocation, arriving meticulously prepared to dominate market confusion and uncertainty. When others freeze up, the masters of private equity draw on their superior data, collected from a target company's sector or competitors, and apply their judgment and express conviction to act. It might be a technological leap nobody else sees or a secular trend invisible to most or a cyclical industry in turmoil. A rival firm is hesitating? Time to convert the inaction of another into profit for your investors and yourself. Some firms call themselves "strategic investors," some consider themselves to be "business partners," while others prefer to be known as "contrarian investors." Each firm has its own flavor of branding and its own description of the investment approach it takes. However, the central tenet is the same: Deal professionals back themselves—with investors' money—to make the tough calls that others cannot or will not make.

What this means in practice is that being a master of private equity means being drawn to complexity. Even embracing this simple trait is itself contrarian. Nowadays, most people want an app to simplify life, to make easier decisions, to "hack" their lives to save time to boost their productivity and for fun personal pursuits. We actively shun complexity. We like simplicity. We like the gig economy, to share and to spread the effort and cost involved in many of the things that we do. Perhaps we have lost investigative skills, and the notion of what is too much effort has shifted backward. Maybe we love quick fixes; some of us expect instant gratification. Private equity folks run hard against this grain—because solving complex problems often yields better investment results. Their mindset is different. They relish a situation to unpack, as that is where some of the biggest profits hide.

Consider the psychology at work. It is the opposite of taking the path of least resistance or accepting the simplest answer. They aren't looking for shortcuts. Private equity investors have an ingrained skepticism, a natural inclination to investigate, question, critique, and deconstruct. They expect wrinkles beneath the surface, and they do not trust easily when a situation looks smooth. This trait is inculcated in private equity foot soldiers, and it is well honed for the few who have reached the top. And they can do this complex work at speed, analyzing multi-billion-dollar assets in weeks, if necessary.

All this work is done by people. There are no machines to punch algorithms, and nothing is automated, from the financial analyses to the debates in the investment committee. This world is driven by people with a mindset to take a personal interest, to make investments, and to help run them until refinancing and exit. Complexity invites choice, and in making the right choices you gain an edge. You do not need to be a finance expert to understand how this contrasts starkly from picking stocks or spreading bets in a mutual fund or making passive investments—however large—only to leave management to work alone. The attraction to complexity is one of the most important mental frameworks and identifiers in private equity.

The investment committee has little appetite for "low-hanging fruit," deals where there is less to do and only through financial engineering will there be any hope of making an acceptable return for their investors. These deals make seasoned private equity folks groan.

Easy wins rarely make an individual's career, let alone a firm's reputation. To make pension fund commitments sticky, to turn the first-time investor into the serial subscriber to fund after fund, across products from buyouts to credit, a private equity firm must have a collection of deals to showcase where they saw something unique, actioned it, and managed the outcome to differentiate themselves. Investments that reveal glimpses of brilliance are the types of trades that get attention on a firm's website.

How does this mindset work? To illustrate it, let's return to the depths of the financial crisis. It took the major central banks and governments of the world several months to stabilize and boost the global economy, and during this time, panic was widespread. Perhaps nowhere was the panic more acute than in the financial services industry, especially among banks and insurers. After the collapse of the insurance company AIG in 2008, it was natural for both insurance policyholders and stockholders to worry whether their insurers could suffer the same fate. What if their life insurance was worthless? Or their home insurance might not pay out? Or their insurance for business interruption, or hurricanes, could not be relied upon? What if their insurer was about to become insolvent?

It seemed as if nearly every insurer was tainted with the same brush as AIG—even if there was little or nothing to substantiate this fear. To most, it seemed nearly impossible to really understand what was happening under the hood of the insurance industry, what the assets of insurers were really valued at and what their liabilities really were—let alone invest in these businesses with other people's money. It was remarkable. A multi-trillion-dollar industry that once looked staid, even boring, full of dull suits and bland ties, had been set on fire. That was when private equity struck.

While others ran for the hills, private equity ran into a burning building.

"I don't love it."

Our opening pitch to the investment committee falls flat when one of the most senior partners registers his lack of interest in moving forward with the deal. It isn't the premise; the Firm is enthusiastic about developing expertise in the same sector—insurance—that one of finance's most disciplined investors, Warren Buffett, used to center his holdings and make deals that were elephant-sized in scale and profit. It is not the transaction pathway; the deal team has recommended buying an underperforming large insurer for a song and turning it around during a severe recession, rather than spend ten years with regulators setting one up from scratch and slowly adding size to the business through acquisitions and organic growth. The problem is the audacity: Investing over a billion dollars in an untested and opaque idea in a visible way, by snapping up a sizable public company when the stock market is perilously choppy and figuring out the right valuation, may be impossible. Is it an ingenious idea or is it absurdly complicated? Some of the other partners decide it is the latter and side with their vocal colleague.

They have a point. General Insurance Group is a notoriously gray company, weak on disclosure despite being publicly listed, and run at the senior level by forgettable executives who are enormously lucky that sleepy stockholders demand so little of them. The business underwrites life and property and casualty insurance through six entities in Chicago, Bermuda, and London, covering both retail customers and wholesale clients via platforms as different as online channels for "moms and pops" and offices for specialized commercial risks. One piece of revenue might come from insuring your aunt's life, whereas another might be for insuring a Gulf oil pipeline against terrorism or cyber-crime, or skyscrapers against hurricanes and other natural disasters. It is a sprawling business built through haphazard organic expansion partly driven by management ego and a lack of planning rather than the desire and skill to be best in class.

Although the financial markets do not focus on General Insurance and its stock price is more or less stuck at the same level it has been for three years, the clear possibility of unforeseen, outsized claims that threaten the solvency of the group is hard to overlook. Unraveling the layers of underwriting across the company will be a giant task. Changing the investment strategy for assets gathered from premiums earned could attract unwelcome attention from regulators and clients.

The business has never faced an existential threat, but are a few grenades lurking beneath the surface? It's hard to tell and easy to worry about—even get paranoid about. The skeptical partners on the Firm's investment committee aren't the only ones who feel this way. Every clever strategic acquirer in the insurance industry has let go of the chance to buy it. What do the Firm's deal team know that the smartest brains in this sector do not? Is the team correct about the potential here? Have they really spotted a smart bargain?

Compounding those worries is the fact of the target fighting back. Every sensitive discussion the deal team has with General Insurance's board is being leaked to the press. It also looks like the company is shopping the terms proposed by the Firm for a potential buyout to the Firm's competitors. Arguments have broken out with the target's management team, who fail to see the point of an investment by private equity—surely, they think, everything they can do to improve the company's prospects is already being done? What do private equity folks know about how to run an insurance business? The atmosphere in negotiations between the Firm and the target is not hostile, but it isn't the most constructive or trusting.

Even if a deal can be struck, such a dynamic can make it hard for the Firm to influence the business once it is under private equity ownership. The deal team is honest and transparent about these issues, and it's clear they will have to work hard to secure the investment committee's approval to strike a deal.

"Remember satellites. This will be bigger."

The deal partner serves an ace. Eleven years ago, when the Founder was still actively originating and executing deals himself, he worked with the same partner on the Firm's first investment in a satellite business. It was unheard of at the time for private equity to invest in the satellite industry; you could not see the assets from Earth, let alone fix them if they went wrong, and the cost of launch failure or malfunction was prohibitive. Investing in the satellite industry, at first blush, was the very definition of complexity. And it's not as if any of the Firm's investment professionals had personal experience with satellites or rockets. They were all trained as financiers. But through original thinking, painstaking due diligence, and relentless negotiation, the Founder discovered a gold mine.

He realized that you could structure insurance protection against the risks of a failed launch, or in-orbit malfunctions, even getting state aid to subsidize the premiums if governments were major clients. He found that revenues could be secured with longer-term contracts, with price indexation every year and clients who tended to renew without fuss to ensure continuity for critical services such as data communications. He pushed operating profit margins in the satellite company to over sixty percent, and with so much surplus free cash flow, lending banks were easily persuaded to permit regular dividends to be paid out from the business back to investors. He educated financing markets about how robust and profitable these assets are, before exiting via a blowout IPO after satellite valuations had more than doubled.

The Founder staked his career in the investment committee on the success of the bet, and it worked. He hit the jackpot. The deal made a profit of ten times the money invested by the private equity fund. It was a signature trade for the Firm and led to other successful deals in the satellite industry, and its rivals spent the next five years in a slow game of catch-up. The Founder made his name as a visionary investor.

The partner, who was the junior resource on the satellite project, is now strategically invoking a past glory to buy the deal team more time in the committee. He knows what the team still needs to do to be convincing: to detail the merits of the investment, to unpack its complexity in micro steps, and to show how, as with satellites, what seemed to be crazy was actually plausible.

The goal of invoking past success is not to flatter the Founder; it is to explain why they should develop a keen appetite for insurance, despite the industry's complexities—because if done correctly, the risks are far outweighed by the returns, within a narrow band of outcomes. And so the deal team tells a story of what the "good" kind of complex looks like, to justify why they are drawn to it—why they are drawn to General Insurance.

The underpinning of their interest is the macro backdrop. The financial crisis is likely to be shorter-lived than the financial markets expect, they believe, because the Federal Reserve is poised to unleash powerful weapons of monetary policy on an unprecedented scale—in coordination with its counterparts overseas. The credit crunch will be overwhelmed by a sea of liquidity. This gift of almost a trillion dollars of freshly printed cash from the Fed alone will lift stock and debt markets to the point that investors will forget the jagged falls and crashes that have been torturing them in recent months. To be blunt, things will not stay cheap for long. It is an excellent time to buy a good business.

General Insurance's operational diversification is also a clear plus. There are ninety different lines in the book, from standard home insurance in one part of the world to hurricane reinsurance somewhere else, and these lines are largely non-correlated. In other words, they are distinct and separate risks. A failure in one business is not likely to trigger failure elsewhere. A property claim on a shipping fleet policy in Canada is not going to precipitate a claim on an entertainment business interruption policy in California. And not only are the lines not correlated with each other, they are also not directly correlated to what is happening in the macro economy. There is some overlap and some moral hazard—as claims tend to go up when money is tight—but this is not a traditional cyclical business that reacts the same way when the rest of the economy is being hit.

In fact, as the deal team sees it, the forces of supply and demand in insurance are favorable, with prices for policies "hardening," or going up, even if the economic picture for other industries has dimmed. Insurers have endured years of heavy claims due to poor underwriting decisions in the past, and this has started to feed into higher prices for new policies. The darkest days have passed. Rates for insuring risk are going up, and this means returns in the industry on underwriting are going up. So, although stock market valuations have tanked across the board, the dip for insurance companies isn't justified by the business fundamentals. This industry is far healthier than Wall Street is giving it credit for. General Insurance has a terrific opportunity to prune and grow its book of policies, backing those that are rising with more capital and pulling out of those that still have weak rates. In other words, the opportunity lies in focusing harder on where the profit is and less in showing off its broad market presence.

Historically, the company has done the opposite. Management panicked when unexpected losses tore apart the annual budget, firing underwriters and exiting insurance and reinsurance lines that were likely to rebound when the industry raised renewal rates to recoup claims. They missed out on higher prices post-losses. Management feared how inhospitable public markets might react to losses or making big bets, and so the underwriters played it safe even in the knowledge that this was the wrong strategy to create profit. They lost their nerve.

As seasoned hunters of wounded prey, the Firm's deal team recognizes the parallel with distressed investing. The key to making underwriting profitable is to invest in writing sound policies when others are fearful, to commit ahead of the market moving up in rates. The Firm has this skill in abundance and can deploy it here too. In private hands, the deal team can help correct management's tendency toward self-inflicted wounds. They can support the star revenue generators to do what they feel would work best, removing for them the distraction of the public markets and research analysts' views. The Firm can help General Insurance refocus, make tough decisions, and emerge from private equity ownership as a more valuable company. The Firm hires a team of twelve actuaries from a leading accounting firm to evaluate and critique the profit and loss assumptions behind every single underwriting position on the insurer's books. The purpose is to check whether what was reserved is reasonable, to see where money can be released from the balance sheet and where money needs to be held back. It is incredibly intensive work, far more detailed than what competitors are likely to do. And this due diligence comes with a hefty price tag: four million dollars on actuaries alone. In fact, the Wall Street bankers advising the two sides on the deal think the project team has gone too far. *Why not just make reasonable assumptions about the actuarial inputs?* they think. It would be accurate "enough." But the Firm does not care and the Founder does not care what anyone else thinks of the approach. They will do things the harder way, and as it turns out the millions of dollars spent on actuaries is money well spent, because their findings support the hypothesis that the business does not have hidden underwriting risks lurking in the shadows. The slate is clean.

To add another level of scrutiny to protect their capital, the team also hires a team of attorneys from a firm specializing in insurance issues to cross-check whether the numbers in each individual insurance contract in the company's books, above a given size threshold, match the numbers used in the actuarial analysis. They're checking if the contracts match the financial models. The lawyers are checking the accountants. The deal team cross-examines both sets of advisors, fielding frequent requests from the Founder for updates at all hours of the day.

The actuarial modeling of each line of insurance runs into hundreds of pages, with each input benefiting from exhaustive interrogations of the business's underwriters. The deal team iterates and debates the financial analysis with such intensity that numbers and spreadsheets fill their nightly dreams. What this multilayered work reveals is priceless. General Insurance has been so conservative that despite there being only a small risk of excessive losses across the group, owing to the company's diversification and anti-risk stance, the business has a three hundred million *surplus* of dollars tucked away in hidden parts of the balance sheet—three hundred million *extra* dollars over and above what it will ever realistically need for claims.

This money can be extracted as a dividend post-acquisition.

The due diligence also suggests that General Insurance's structure of six underwriting entities can be slimmed down to just two and that some of the business can be moved online. There is no need to have six entities sourcing insurance and reinsurance—other than for the incumbent CEO to feel like he is the big boss of a public company. The business can achieve the same degree of diversification with a cheaper, more efficient operating structure, in which it will be easier to spot underwriting mistakes as well as reward and incentivize good employees. A bit of dismantling will also release capital that is tied up in the convoluted structure, meaning that more money can be invested for organic growth, or "liberated" as a dividend.

On top of the potential for restructuring the business, there are significant bloated costs to trim. General Insurance is paying for expensive sponsorship deals with sports teams that offer little benefit. It needlessly maintains two Gulfstream private jets. Some managers work four days a week because their workloads are perennially light. Bonus plans have targets that are far too easy to meet. Pensions are inexplicably overfunded, and the company's contributions to pension programs can be scaled back to the lower end of targets set by regulators. The IT department is overstaffed and full of pet projects that the business will never realize value from. Low-grade IT can be outsourced to Asia.

The attractions of General Insurance do not stop there.

General Insurance is sitting on three billion dollars, money known in the insurance trade as the "float." These assets are client premiums held against possible claims. Management is simply holding this sum in cash, which is earning nothing, or in sovereign debt. The Firm can do much better with this untapped reservoir by managing the three billion dollars directly, in a mix of the Firm's credit funds and selected external money managers that the Firm rates highly. The extra yield that can be generated from the assets this way will add to General Insurance's profitability and value.

As the investment committee realizes the potential of securing the assets for direct management, some of the once-skeptical eyes in the investment committee start to light up. The private equity business has found a deal where the credit business would also benefit—justifiably, and at good scale. Of course, the assets will be managed on arm's-length terms and will be subject to approval by the target's new board. This board will be appointed by and composed of the deal team plus independent non-executives chosen by the Firm.

What else can be done with the target? General Insurance is

debt-free, and so the deal team looks at a creative way of issuing a high-yield bond. This is a novel strategy within the insurance industry, which is generally averse to low-grade credit. However, now is the time to strike, as interest rates are close to zero and debt investors are desperate for yield, even if only some of the interest is paid in cash. Rolling up half of the interest payments as a promise to pay the debt investors in the future ("payment-in-kind" interest) means passing some of this debt obligation on to the next owner of the business many years from now. If the credit markets are frothy enough to accept it, why not? And by structuring this junk debt above the perimeter of operations directly governed by industry regulators, there is freer rein to price and size the offering to the biggest bond that the company can comfortably afford. The money raised will finance a large dividend.

Taken together, the dividends from restructuring and refinancing the target as described above will return over fifty percent of the money initially invested to buy General Insurance within twelve months.

In the investment committee meeting, the deal team also highlights a favorable clause in the private equity fund documents between the Firm and its investors that permits any money returned within a year to be invested again on other deals. This neat trick, known as "recycling," means that the Firm can boost the size of its private equity fund by counting twice any monies returned within that time frame as available for investment. In other words, if, say, five hundred million dollars are returned within a year from the General Insurance deal, this sum can be reinvested by the Firm as if it were fresh money from the investors. That's five hundred million dollars more to make a profit on, and earn performance fees on if the money is invested well.

By now the tide is turning, and sentiment on the project has grown more positive. Here is a big target trading at a low valuation in a regulated business where the barriers to entry are thick and numerous. The Firm can invest a billion-dollar equity check in a sector not linked directly to other investments in the private equity fund, in a target that is managed without conviction. There is so much that can be done with this company; there are so many levers to pull to create value. There are very good executives who are worth promoting, and others who can go. It looks and feels like a good private equity deal.

If it makes this flagship investment, the Firm will become a pioneer in a complex industry that requires specialist expertise. The investment in due diligence by the Firm on General Insurance, from the actuaries to the insurance attorneys to its own internal financial analysis and strategic thinking, puts the Firm miles ahead of its rivals. They will still wonder what the Firm is doing in the insurance industry, while the deal team will be stuck into portfolio management—and plotting the next insurance deal. Investors will credit the Firm as the innovator of an original idea later copied across the private equity industry, and competitors will envy the Firm's savvy. There's really a lot to like.

If the deal is a success and General Insurance emerges from private equity ownership as a more profitable, better capitalized company, the Firm will also have earned the respect and the trust of the regulators in the insurance industry, who until now have had very little contact with private equity firms as investors of insurance businesses—and are likely to be skeptical about them. Being the first mover in insurance will confer this advantage on the Firm, too. And this advantage will come in handy if the Firm builds out its insurance business in years to come.

All of this is there for the taking, if the Firm's investment committee agrees that the building is not on fire—it is the neighborhood that is burning. The building—General Insurance—is intrinsically strong, if unloved, and it will thrive, if taken care of. The neighborhood—the insurance industry in the wake of AIG's collapse—has covered this target with a smokescreen of complexity that the deal team has worked hard to look through. What General Insurance needs is someone to come along and see its value, to unlock its potential. It needs private equity. The key changes required in the business are never going to happen by themselves. The deal team has already put in hundreds of man-hours of effort, working seven days a week, to reveal the target's worth. A new handpicked management team is on standby, each hire a rock star who has gotten the memo about the essentials of the business plan that lies ahead. What once looked insurmountable now looks . . . achievable.

Moments later, with a final nod of the Founder's head, a billion-dollar investment in insurance is approved.

We can think of the "good complexity" that attracts the masters of private equity as a path to value creation that is hidden to most. The hidden part is what makes it complicated. The good part is that once it is discovered, the path is paved with gold. With the insurance deal, as with the satellite deal before it, private equity investors considered new projects that at first looked like odd ideas, seemingly out of left field, but in truth they had an underlying logic to them that was cold and rational, and a plan that led to a multiple of the money invested.

That private equity professionals solve complex problems so much of the time is proof that they can do what many other types of investor cannot do. This attraction to complexity is not exclusive to the industry, but it is commonplace among private equity firms, and it is a fundamental part of their reason for being. In our sketch, the insurance investment was not a binary bet on a set of events, such as whether there would be a light or heavy hurricane season in the Atlantic, or an unprincipled roll of the dice on making changes to a business that were hard to fathom. It was a complex situation that was taken apart by the deal team, who broke it down into levers that would control whether value was created or destroyed and then organized a method of attack. The stars were forced to align, until the deal looked almost easy—in hindsight, it does look easy.

Right now, the masters of private equity are executing even more complex trades involving technological changes or developments in life sciences. Their enthusiasm for investing in new sectors with unique angles has almost no limit. In hindsight, these investments will look sensible and perhaps even obvious in part. What makes them tough is the hard calls that need to be made before it becomes obvious that they should be made. It is this kind of thinking and action that investors in private equity funds have come to rely on, and it's a big part of why they keep coming back with commitments.

It is not that the masters of private equity take big risks to boost deal returns; it is that their calculus of risks is different. They do enough work to establish that the risks are *worth taking* because the reward is *at least commensurate* and believe that the outcome is *achievable*. They go through a mind map of what could happen with an investment, analyzing what is required for a deal to be successful. It is painstaking work.

Of course, the result is uncertain, and the journey is a gamble, albeit one made on the basis of confidence in their judgment being largely correct. That it is correct most of the time is what generates consistent investment results.

How does the aspiring master of private equity develop this mindset toward complexity, acceptable risk, and adequate return? It comes down to a set of characteristics that can be based on both natural aptitude and learned experience:

- the willingness to embrace and investigate the unknown, or even chaos—or at least the absence of identifiable order;
- the drive to develop and execute a logical plan to understand whether a sector is suitable for investment, and how to structure that investment to achieve the best risk/return;
- the humility to admit what you do not know, to clarify what you need to believe about a deal in order to commit investors' money to it—and to own up to error and try to fix mistakes;
- the insatiable appetite to find a good business and figure out how to make it even better;
- the understanding of whether the changes a business needs to be successful are realistic and achievable, regardless of whether they are difficult;
- the mix of patience and intellectual curiosity to dig for data to analyze and the conviction to base decisions to create value on that data and your judgment;
- the emotional intelligence and empathy to realize that the folks who are going to do the hardest work to create value during the life of an investment are on the shop floor—the management and employees of a business—and how to identify and partner with them.

When private equity professionals look at where a target is at the start of a deal and compare this to how they expect the target to increase in value during private equity ownership, these are the factors they focus on. As they observe the increase in value of an investment and the risk of things going wrong, they ask themselves, week in and week out, *Can I see this working out?*

In 2020 and 2021, the period in which I was writing this book, burning buildings were everywhere—and the masters of private equity were running inside. Private equity dealmakers analyzed the risks of businesses impacted by the Covid-19 pandemic, positively and negatively, uncovering concrete paths to compelling returns across the economy. Often, such deals involved structuring the money going in as loans, or a mix of loans and equity, or a hybrid instrument such as preferred equity that has attributes of both. Money was invested in airlines, travel, and car rental franchises with household names, even when almost nobody was traveling, in anticipation of recovery. Money was also invested in sectors that were more active during the crisis, such as life sciences, including hospitals and drug development. As during the financial crisis over a decade earlier, the activity of private equity during the pandemic is an example of navigating complexity.

In each of these cases, private equity folks stepped up. The rise of debt-like investing by private equity firms has highlighted the replacement of traditional lending banks as credit providers. Private equity has captured this white space in part because banks have found such lending more cumbersome in the wake of the financial crisis. In many of these situations, without private equity the investments might never have been made.

The masters of private equity are some of the only investors willing to commit with certainty to the complexity of problematic investments at times, particularly at scale when the deal checks run into the hundreds of millions, if not billions, of dollars—and during harsh macro environments. Government grants or loans are a cheaper source of capital but are rarely available. Cheap debt from lending banks is sometimes not on the table.

Neither alternative would provide the intense partnership with management of portfolio companies that private equity exemplifies, or the focus on business, or the familiarity with complexity and the understanding of how to master it. And what we must accept when we note the growth of private capital and acknowledge its benefits is that the terms on which it is offered are more expensive and more onerous than other sources of money. The more that private equity makes the market, the more it will be able to influence the terms. It is now axiomatic that private equity will demand double-digit annual rates of investment return. Investors need it. Companies accept it.

The single-minded focus on results is one of the traits that private equity investors have perfected to power through the complexity of the deals they examine. We focus on this trait in the next chapter, for it throws fresh light on important features about how the industry works. It reveals how compensation and alignment of incentives with investors are clearly linked to the focus on results. But it also sheds light on some of the reasons why private equity deals can go wrong.

# CHAPTER SIX

# There Is No Formula

"You will make at least $100 million as a partner."

It is past midnight, and the two junior members of the Food-mart deal team are joking around as they work in Excel. The target company is a U.S. food retail chain, and they are updating the financial model for its leveraged buyout by the flagship private equity fund managed by the Firm. The young men are in their early and late twenties, respectively. Each was hired by the Firm after graduating from Wharton and completing two years at Goldman Sachs in the investment banking division. They are reminiscing about the orientation program speech given during their first week at the Firm by the former head of Human Resources, an impressive but insecure executive who, rumor had it, had organized his own surprise birthday parties.

The HR head had given the same speech to both associates, with the same "$100 million" line, despite their joining three years apart. The quote was accurate, and it reflected how earning this kind of money used to be addressed up front with new recruits as one of the benefits of a long and successful career at the Firm. That was before the Firm's IPO.

Things changed when the Firm went public, and compensation was now part of the growing list of delicate topics that were not to be discussed openly. Still, the pair cannot help but keep the promise of wealth in mind now and then as they crunch the numbers ahead of the Foodmart presentation to the investment committee. It's wealth they can't really imagine, even though they are surrounded by it (and multiples of it) every day.

Though the pair works hard, they know many are skeptical of their chosen profession. At parties, some of their college friends don't hesitate to launch into the popular accusations thrown at private equity, that the deals make a lot of money but do not create much value and so forth. The deal team duo has heard the narrative many times by now, and it goes something like this: Private equity investors target vulnerable companies to buy, saddle them with debt, cut costs to the bone, and sell for a quick profit. It is financial engineering—private equity is the house flipper of the financial world. If any operating improvements are made to the business, they are superfluous to the primary goal: getting out quick for a tidy profit. Private equity follows a fixed and predictable investment method.

Despite their limited time in private equity jobs, the young men already know that this version of events is nonsense. Every hour of their working days and nights proves it. Private equity managers do not debate business plans for companies in the investment committee that would fit on the back of a paper napkin. They do not stake investors' money or their careers on selfish schemes to extract cash and pass on the leftovers to the next buyer. They are not so naïve as to think they can charge their fees and take their profit shares on the basis of myopic, half-baked ideas. That is not the way to create a sustainable investment business, and they know it. They see it at work every day.

Each private equity firm has its own version of a playbook, with techniques that have been proven over multiple investments, including preferred blends of operational and financial changes to consider making to target companies. Each partner will have war stories and lessons learned about how past projects went right or wrong. But in truth, these tools are only guides, not guaranteed means to win. Each project starts with a strategic vision and an operating plan for the target, and either this blueprint or a revised version that accounts for new circumstances forms the core of the next few years' work to create value in the business. Adding leverage to the target is only one part of it. The strategy will have to be evidenced as backable to achieve a lucrative exit.

The next owners of a business targeted by private equity, whether the public markets or another private equity fund or a corporate buyer, are unlikely to pay up for a target that has been window-dressed. Those buyers will quantify the operational and financial progress made during the ownership by private equity, and they are not going to be persuaded if the only work done was to issue high-yield bonds, cut costs, and pay out dividends.

For the masters of private equity, there is no fixed formula. Rather, to be successful, the investment professionals must stay focused on the band of returns that each deal should make as compensation for its risks—and pivot the company as an instrument to achieve this goal. What counts is training the mind to keep the objective in view, even if the territory is uncertain. If circumstances demand, they might even have to throw out the strategy and operating plan that the investment committee originally approved and start over. Or they might replace what looked like the right management team and board of directors due to performance or personality issues, bringing in fresh executives and non-executive board members. It can be anything. Whatever it takes to get the result for investors.

The key trait, which the two young men on the Foodmart

deal team are learning, is having a single-minded focus on the outcome combined with the flexibility and creativity to get there. They cannot afford to flinch. And whether the project is to buy the target company or invest in its debt, the associates know that their deal team has power over the company's board and influence over the business that matches how the money is invested—buying it outright or lending to it or some combination of methods. They have the capacity to forge and refine the shape and trajectory of the enterprise. They have the attention of management. They are active money managers, more so than any other type of asset manager. They have the financial motive to succeed, and they have an unfettered opportunity to try. The project is a blank canvas upon which to craft a lucrative story, and so at exit, the target will take the form of the best available opportunity to realize profit.

Our two junior associates have learned by now that keeping the deal returns at the top of their minds is key. The math of how much profit is expected for investors and for the Firm is etched into them. They will recalibrate the sensitivity of returns to positive surprises and negative shocks. They will monitor the growth in the target's profits and cash flow. They will keep an eye on the time frame and the options for exit. And everyone on the team will have a rough idea of how much money they stand to make from the deal, including carried interest.

So, our aspiring masters of private equity know that it does not matter if the walls of the deal maze around them are moving; it only matters that they have (or quickly gain) the ability and stamina to craft a worthwhile exit. Let's take a closer look at how this might play out in a deal, in this case an investment that experienced big problems.

\*    \*    \*

It is 2020. The U.S. economy is weak, kept afloat by government spending and favorable policy moves by the Fed, while consumer and industrial activity gradually awaken from pandemic-induced recession. There will be little clarity on the macro picture for the economy for at least two years. The financial markets cracked during the downturn and are still healing as I write this. In this gloomy setting, the Firm acquires a food retailer serving the middle class. It makes sense; people always need to eat at home.

Foodmart provides groceries and household staples at affordable prices in inexpensive cities across the country. The business, long owned by a single family, had been facing a crisis of leadership as the aging founders were looking to retire without a viable successor in the family. It also needs to modernize in response to online competition. Bankers conduct an auction, but the Firm's deal partner, who is close to the family, having built a relationship with them spanning many years, has the inside track. The Firm is well placed to lead worthwhile operational changes at Foodmart given the Firm's track record of investments in the food retail sector and network of contacts at suppliers, logistics providers, and consumer goods multinationals. It seems like a great fit. The Firm's deal partner agrees to the founding family's request to retain a fifteen percent stake to share in future upside, and he negotiates a controlling investment by the private equity fund.

The target is acquired during a period of slow-moving turmoil. The Foodmart stores are popular with a loyal middle-class clientele, but they have aged and are somewhat down-market. Affluent white-collar young people tend to shop elsewhere, even if they have to pay higher prices. The company's stodgy brand does not appeal to them. The look and feel of the group is stagnant. The Firm's partner is of the opinion that the company is at risk of becoming a slow-melting ice cube, and to counter this fate, he plans to make changes that will lift prices and margins by upgrading the stores, revamping the customer proposition, and overhauling the marketing. The business is set to transition upmarket within three years. A new online offering, backed with investments in technology and logistics, rounds out the strategic vision for Foodmart.

The Firm also believes that the former owners significantly undervalued a key part of the target. The company's real estate portfolio, its network of stores and warehouses, was accumulated forty years ago at low prices. The parcels are wholly owned, many in desirable urban neighborhoods that have gentrified in recent years. Given a rise in commercial property prices in recent decades, that footprint is a gold mine, perhaps worth as much as the operating business itself. The founding family did not consider selling the property because this went against their "American Dream" ideals. *Never sell your property,* they used to say.

But the Firm, not encumbered by this kind of straitjacket thinking, begins to analyze how to split the group into an operating entity (the "opco") and a property entity (the "propco"). Part of the overnight work the deal team juniors are doing is to estimate the extra profit that could be generated by restructuring the property portfolio in this way, in parallel with the store transformation. The team considers two options: selling the property in pieces to the highest bidder and leasing back the retail space or leveraging the parcels to eighty percent of their current market value. There is no shortage of attractive bids for the sites, and Wall Street banks are eager to lend at rock-bottom interest rates.

The Firm selects the latter option—leveraging the sites—as the investment committee believes the real estate will continue to increase in value, and the lending banks will permit nearly all of the proceeds from borrowing against the property to finance a dividend. The dividend is so large that the entire equity check from the fund for the leveraged buyout is paid back within six months. What this means is that every dollar returned to the fund from the investment after this point is profit for the investors and carried interest for the Firm—as the saying goes, "The rest is all upside." This result permits the deal partner to embrace the business transformation with extra zeal, because the investors' money has already been returned.

However, after twelve months, it is clear that the operational changes at Foodmart are not faring so well. The deal team had anticipated some of the issues, such as dissatisfaction in communities where stores have been shuttered because the newly installed management team does not think the upmarket transition will work. The deal partner expects that these issues will fade as other retailers move into the impacted areas. The trickier problem is that affluent young people are not flocking to the refurbished stores as expected, and the data does not show any sign of improvement.

There is a clear reason for this problem, and it is not going to be temporary. The food retail sector has experienced an earthquake. A direct competitor to Foodmart has been acquired in a surprise move by an online consumer goods giant, which has adopted a strategy of keeping the stores but also offering premium and basic groceries and household goods online with free delivery across the nation. It is working. Customers of all backgrounds are drawn to their portal and click with ease to complete their weekly shopping. Foodmart's nascent online offering can't compete. The online giant, possessing financial firepower and logistics resources that dwarf even that of the world's largest private equity funds, starts to cut prices on fresh produce from bread to avocados and on household goods from soap to toilet paper. It's going for the kill, and nobody saw this coming.

The situation is dangerous, and without pivoting, Foodmart will likely join a long list of brick-and-mortar retail casualties of the evolution to online shopping. The company urgently needs to redefine its reason to exist. Bond investors start to dump the high-yield debt issued by Foodmart for its leveraged buyout, and the price of this paper falls to seventy cents on the dollar. The Firm must act.

The deal partner tasks the company's management team with harvesting within sixty days a stream of live data from Foodmart's stores and its loyalty card customers detailing which products are popular and which are not, as well as what the business can offer beyond its rivals' reach, especially that of the new online competitor. The team surveys opinions, reexamines prices across the market, and negotiates with suppliers to find smarter and cheaper ways to source quality produce. The Firm brings in former executives from the food retail sector to cross-check the data for guidance. A panel of consultants plays Devil's advocate to ensure the decisions that might result are thoroughly vetted.

And the data tells an intuitive story. Shopping online is easier, but it lacks the essential touch of the in-store experience, which is more important when shopping for fresh produce rather than packaged goods. Customers like to shop for "everyday luxuries"—basic foods of better quality where the source and method of making are a little kinder to their bodies and to the environment—so long as they are not breaking the bank. They want to buy their families a better product, and a knowledgeable and motivated store assistant can be helpful to have on hand. They do not entirely trust that fresh produce bought online is always fresh and that the items they receive are likely to be the same that they would have chosen themselves in a store. Customers value loyalty as a two-way street; they are willing to pay a little more but want to be rewarded for it. Folks also want to feel part of a community, and in return they will be sticky and spread the good word.

The deal team decides to shoot for a quantum leap because the current strategy isn't working. They have to move fast, start moving pieces around the chessboard even if their revised strategy for Foodmart is still a work in progress. They decide to pivot the business toward the data collected rather than wait to finalize the ideal way forward. The perfect is the enemy of the good.

Changing an investment thesis is easy to describe and difficult to do. In the high-stakes environment of private equity, it can seem hard at first to admit failure, to admit error in front of colleagues, many of whom are alpha types. There is the fear of losing respect, and the fear of being viewed as not a good (enough) investor. These fears are magnified because of the concentration of power, the tightness of the circle of those in charge, and the open-plan nature of the investment committee, where juniors can witness partners rise or fall by their decisions and leadership. Each person is visible; each individual is attached to the deals they are responsible for. There is nowhere to hide.

The Foodmart deal partner accepts the challenge and makes the case to the investment committee. Foodmart must rebrand, create a community around the concept of fresh produce, shore up its loyalty program, and focus on independent and small suppliers. Although in-store prices will be higher, customers will be able to see and touch the value of shopping in the store. The business will ditch the aspiration to be upmarket, and reorient to attracting all types of customers, providing an in-store experience that's worth the trip to the store. This means free tastings of premium produce and free premium recycled paper bags at checkout. It means store assistants packing your groceries and making worthwhile recommendations on in-season produce. Shopping in-store will be something to enjoy, not endure.

"How can you be sure that will work *this time*?"

It is part of the deal partner's job to deflect loaded questions and comments from skeptical colleagues. The atmosphere in the investment committee is tense, a dose of mea culpa mixed with the conviction the deal team must demonstrate to secure approval. It is part of the Firm's job to be both constructive and cautious and to support the deal team with suggestions even if it sometimes comes across as deeply critical. For the juniors watching from the edges of the boardroom, the experience can feel a little like a civilized form of blood sport. And these days, pounding the table helps a lot less than it might have done a decade ago. Crisp and thoughtful replies backed up by numbers are more likely to persuade than a raised voice.

Two hours later, the Firm settles on a way forward. The investment committee endorses a new strategic vision for Foodmart, with the expected profits from the new business plan at least as big as originally underwritten, even if they are now projected to take a few years longer to crystallize. Foodmart will be rebranded "Farm-Fresh," a label that speaks of fresh produce at everyday prices from proprietary suppliers. Everything is fresh, or nearly fresh, and is organic, or nearly organic. The company will be presented as a farm-to-table offering, with produce from earnest local agricultural folks who trust Farm-Fresh to sell their goods. Prices will be kept moderate, although more expensive zip codes will pay a little extra, which nobody minds too much. The loyalty program will give generous cashback offers to customers who do nearly all of their regular shopping at the store. Nothing about the company will smack of Wall Street.

The strategy pivot is a runaway success. Farm-Fresh cultivates a green halo, loyalty memberships skyrocket, and the business looks and feels more like a community than a portfolio investment. Towns that lack a store even petition to have one opened. The deal team has struck the crest of a positive wave, featuring antipathy toward the Big Tech parent of Farm-Fresh's rival, a keen interest in whole and nutritious foods, and a rediscovered interest in close-knit neighborhoods. Small-scale suppliers do not negotiate as hard as larger ones, and so the group is able to drive profits hard while keeping each part of the company's ecosystem happy enough. A year later, Farm-Fresh goes public, and the stock price booms.

And when the ebb and flow of the pandemic forces certain stores to shut temporarily, the deal team plays a masterstroke. Home delivery is introduced for free for active loyalty program customers, facilitated by the main technology and logistics sector rivals to the online giant that now owns Farm-Fresh's competitor. Groceries are fresh and arrive on time, and the company is increasingly seen as a community utility during the waves of lockdowns. The stock climbs a further thirty percent, and the Firm gradually starts to offload its shares in a series of sell-down transactions. Within two years, the Firm realizes a total return of more than triple the money invested.

Throughout the change in strategy, the deal team views the investment through one overriding lens: the expected return to investors versus the risk to their capital of staying invested. The switch from upmarket-focused retailer to organic retailer for all customers is a major rethink, based on data and the views of industry experts—and lived experience. The competition is better funded and, in the event of a price war, could outspend Farm-Fresh multiple times over. But what the company has in its corner is a single-minded owner, quick to recalibrate and tactical in nature, who treats the situation like hand-to-hand combat in a pressurized environment. This is private equity at its best. There's little doubt that Foodmart could have been lost to the online giant if it was not for private equity.

What is the Firm's cut for this work? The check invested in Farm-Fresh is three hundred million dollars, and the money that comes out is over nine hundred million dollars. That's over six hundred million dollars of profit from a successful investment. The Firm's investors are overjoyed with this result. The profit share and fees taken by the Firm for its work exceed one hundred million dollars. The Firm's public shareholders receive about half of this amount through distributions. The other half is invested in the Firm and distributed to the investment professionals. The Founder is the Firm's largest stockholder, and he invests what he receives in his personal portfolio of technology investments and in his modern art collection.

What is striking about the Foodmart sketch is the big difference made by a handful of individuals running the investment. The deal team had to reassess quickly, gather data, and revise its thesis. In a rigid corporate structure, it would not have been possible to deliver such empowerment and speed for investors. You do not run into a firefight by committee. The individuals responsible for the deal ate a little bit of humble pie and continued, undaunted, knowing that the Firm would have their back. They were all in it together.

The foundation of the collective incentive to succeed for both the investors and the Firm is the alignment of their economic incentives. The more investors make, the more the Firm makes and the more the investment professionals take home. So the smarter private equity managers are, the more often they get deals right and the harder they work—the more they succeed at their jobs—the more everyone gets. What private equity earns is a function of what the investors make. This is a big part of why they are laser-focused on the outcome of each investment.

Of course, things do not always work out well. Most firms can cite examples of deals that went off the rails—deals where, despite having the alignment of economics and a clear aim on the objective, the net result was little or no return after several years or even a loss of capital. Sometimes, the deal team can be so close to the firefight and so focused on the objective that they lose critical perspective. They can misread the situation. They are in too deep. And a frequent reason for this blind spot is that they are missing one of the other ingredients for success that we will discuss shortly.

If this happens, the behavior of investment professionals can go awry. They are aligned on economics with investors but can lose some of the transparency with each other that is critical to collective success. They can fail to be brutally honest about how the deal is really going. In the investment committee, scenarios for expected return presented by the deal team can be skewed toward overly positive, unrealistic outcomes. The downside case is really an upside case airbrushed with sleight of hand; the true downside case would be far worse. Unfortunately, this is precisely what the Firm's partner in our sketch experienced on their next investment.

Let's fast-forward to twelve months after the successful exit from Farm-Fresh, to the deal team's new target in a similar sector.

*   *   *

The investment committee is vigorously debating a three-hundred-million-dollar bet on turning around a food retailer in continental Europe that had been carved out of an international food and consumer goods conglomerate. The deal was supposed to be the second example in quick succession of how the Firm creates value for investors in a complex situation in food retail where operational changes are needed, but the investment has gone wrong somewhere.

The strategic vision is familiar and is based on the Farm-Fresh experience: Sell fresh, locally sourced food and organic household goods at reasonable prices to all customer segments and create a sense of community around the brand. The seller tried to improve the target's operations for a decade but gave up after a series of unsatisfactory management changes. With the retailer now owned by the Firm's private equity fund, the Farm-Fresh deal partner is confident that he can do better. Consultants help rebrand the company "Organic Foods" soon after the investment is completed. Although early sales data is positive, progress soon stalls. A year later, the project is materially behind budget, and the gap is growing fast.

New data from the store network and customers is worrying. The brand is seen as a passing fad with a manicured image. Independent suppliers prefer working with local stores in European markets such as France and Germany, rather than a chain owned by U.S.-based private equity. The makeover has failed to persuade customers, and the refurbished stores are nearly empty. When the investment committee reviews the numbers, the partners' reaction is a mix of concern and fury. They want to help, but they are dismayed at how wrong they all appear to be on this investment, so early in the investment period. One of the most tenacious private equity professionals in the meeting makes an indelicate remark. It is meant to sting.

"I guess one deal does not make us experts."

Having taken a hit to his pride, the deal partner defends the team—and himself—for ten minutes, without pause, recounting his track record over decades like a commercial for his résumé. The facts he cites about past deals are correct, but they are also not germane to the present situation. His monologue is a bad move—and not because past performance is no guarantee of future performance. The little lecture smacks of ego, of a know-it-all attitude, of desperation. Above all, he has reacted wildly without thinking through that what is being questioned is the judgment on this investment, and the correct reply is simply the best way to fix it. It was a barbed comment, not a personal attack, but the pressure of being successful has blinded him.

The deal partner requests that more money be invested in the company to shore up liquidity. He ignores well-intentioned advice from some members of the investment committee to split the asset into smaller geographical components for disposal. He insists on firing the same management team that he once argued was perfect for the job. He plans to poach rivals' key executives, knowing they will be expensive. He complains about food retail competitors colluding against Organic. He discusses rosy scenarios for how much profit can be made. He has convinced himself that he can deliver the returns that he promised. He fails to respond directly to the questions he is being asked—instead, he fires off rockets in a crude counterattack at those who ask them. He pauses for air and scans the boardroom for signs of support.

There are none. He has lost the group. Having sat through the deal partner's flailing performance in silence, the Founder finally speaks, offering a few polite words, ending with a soft directive to take the matter offline.

Forty-eight hours later, in a smaller group comprised only of the most senior partners and the Founder, the deal partner continues the discussion on Organic. Now calmer, he persuades the Founder to give him an opportunity to turn things around, but he is granted only a limited chance. A slimmed-down action plan is approved, with the requirement to report back on a shorter leash than is customary. New management is hired and sets about making changes that they insist are more likely to work than the original strategy. They try to make the stores look and feel more local. They focus more on low prices to attract customers. It's an admirable effort

But these moves do not work, no matter how hard or how quickly they are made or how many times the business is made to pivot. And rather than try to change tack, or admit he needs help, the deal partner digs in, playing for more time as he runs out of new ideas. Updates to the investment committee are given less often, and although he does not lie or mislead his colleagues outright, he starts to indulge in "controlled disclosure" about progress. He develops something of a bunker mentality.

After twelve months of going nowhere, the investment committee loses patience and takes over the deal more directly. Organic is sold to a special-purpose acquisition company (or SPAC) listed on local stock exchanges. A SPAC is a cash box with a blank check raised from investors to buy a business within a set timeframe as determined by the executives who run the vehicle. Often, as the vehicle is publicly listed, a SPAC can strike a deal at a higher purchase price than a private equity firm would be willing to pay. Its investors will accept a lower return than they would from a private equity fund, often because the investment is marketed to them as a safer or more straightforward bet. In this case, the SPAC is run by a former senior executive of a French food retail chain and a major hedge fund seeking to expand into the private equity industry. Their joint sector and finance experience is convincing enough for the SPAC's investors to agree that the transaction is likely to be worthwhile.

The price paid is enough for the Firm to get back the money invested by the private equity fund into Organic, but no more. The project has consumed two years of resources, and in this time, investors in the fund have forked over ten million dollars in management fees and one-off transaction fees for the journey. Accounting for those fees, investors have lost money on the investment.

The irony is that the SPAC then does what critics of private equity expected to happen to Organic under the Firm's stewardship. After a short review, during which the failure of the two previous owners was noted, the SPAC team breaks up the business into pieces by geography and sells them to food retail competitors one at a time. The buyers create meaningful synergies by slashing headcount and investments in the store network. This carve-up of the assets takes two years to complete, and although there is no grand strategic vision to be proud of at the end, the SPAC investors are more than happy with their forty percent gain on the investment.

The deal partner at the Firm had discarded a break-up path for Organic while clutching at straws trying to improve the investment, because to him it looked like failure. He wanted to deliver the multiple of money he had promised to others—and to himself. He wanted another great deal story like Farm-Fresh. He was intensely focused, but he reacted to events with a mix of fear and anger rather than getting out in front of them.

In the heat of the deal, he also forgot that the business had important stakeholders beyond the investors: employees, local communities, and suppliers. He managed to get the investors' capital out, and he remained a multimillionaire, but the folks in the company stocking shelves and working the registers were left unimpressed by private equity. As one worker remarked, it would have been better to stay hidden in the aisles under their old corporate owners than go backward under private equity and then get chopped up and sold bit by bit.

In the next chapter, we focus on a trait missing in this deal partner's actions that is crucial for the masters of private equity: the importance of responding to events, rather than reacting to them. Alongside being focused and flexible in method, taking ownership, and embracing complexity, it is another pillar of the private equity path to success.

# CHAPTER SEVEN

# Never React, Always Respond

"Sometimes, being yourself is not a winning strategy."

Sitting in front of a TV camera while a makeup person dabs his forehead, the Founder recollects the words of one of his mentors with a smile. He was a financial titan who had built a powerful and lucrative investment firm before a lengthy ban from the securities industry for insider trading and a short prison sentence ended his career. He emerged from incarceration to devote the rest of his life to philanthropy and politics, a transformation that did not convince some of his critics. He was perhaps not the ideal role model, but his advice was always crisp and helpful to recall at the right moment.

The CNBC cameras are about to roll for the Founder's first interview in Davos, Switzerland. Like other billionaires in asset management, he attends the World Economic Forum every year, but until now he has declined all invitations to speak. It was smarter to maintain his aura; let the bankers and politicians talk, and absorb the atmosphere and feel which way the winds of sentiment were headed. But this time is different, and it is in his interest to be vocal as well as visible.

The Firm has endured an *annus horribilis* in which unwelcome noise about a few of the partners overshadowed another strong year of performance for the flagship private equity, credit, real estate, and infrastructure funds. The mix of issues involved was toxic, involving breaches of regulations uncovered by the Securities and Exchange Commission, a tax investigation by the IRS, and allegations of inappropriate workplace conduct. Although each of the individuals involved was cleared of formal wrongdoing, the noise was unwelcome, not only at the Firm but also for its investors, some of whom decided to pause on making new commitments to the Firm's funds. Each of these issues would have been manageable on its own, but taken together, they have the potential to compound into a reputational crisis. Somewhat crudely, a handful of the Founder's greatest rivals cannot help themselves from making public comparisons between the relatively error-free conduct of their own firms and the seemingly error-prone conduct of the Firm.

This kind of problematic attention is particularly unhelpful in the aftermath of Covid-19, when a new Democratic Party administration in Washington is looking at ways to both improve the public finances, in the wake of income and job support measures deployed during the pandemic, and to address worsening issues of social justice, including wealth inequality. Certain members of the administration appear to have the private equity industry in their sights—specifically, the question of whether income and capital gains taxation for private equity executives is pitched at the right level.

To turn back the tide of sentiment, the Firm embarked on a public relations blitz, highlighting the good work it does for pension funds and other investors, but until now that has not been enough to quiet the critics and soften the news flow. The odd leak to the media about the issues, leading to articles in *The New York Times* and on Bloomberg, detracts further from the Firm's central message that its people act as good citizens as well as good investors.

It is in this context, as the largest stockholder and CEO, that the Founder is stepping into the spotlight in an attempt to seize control of the narrative and refocus the story on the future. The Founder is taking to the airwaves to turn market attention to what the Firm is up to and where it is headed, not to be defensive. Inside, he is burning to defend the Firm—to defend himself— against the negative press he views as blips in an otherwise flawless track record of *being better actors than many others* on Wall Street. *There are so many folks out there far worse than us,* the Founder thinks, and the media should look at our good conduct over decades, not only at these events. But he is self-aware enough to know how badly this would come across in both the mainstream press and on social media, especially given the polarized climate in politics and society. Better to acknowledge past problems in order to tackle and shape the Firm's agenda.

In response to questions from the CNBC anchor, the Founder speaks in plain English with the quiet confidence of a self-made, unflappable winner. He talks as if he is revealing part of a grand plan, hoping that the audience will feel lucky and excited to be let in on what to expect next from the Firm.

"Our industry is in transition," he explains, smiling. "Firms like ours are no longer small, private partnerships. We are now an important part of the financial system, delivering above-market long-term investment returns to folks who need it over a long horizon. Like retirees. We do not track the market. We are not Fidelity or Vanguard. For each unit of risk that we take on, we deliver to our investors a larger unit of return than they can get anywhere else, over a time period that matches the obligations they have. We have made key changes to our internal governance to put this episode behind us. And at five hundred billion dollars of assets under management entrusted to us, I think we are only just getting started."

The two of them—the TV anchor and the Founder—know that critical constituents of the financial ecosystem are watching the broadcast, from policymakers to regulators to investors, and those viewers will dissect each of the Founder's words in order to decipher their meaning. And what the Founder has correctly wagered is that by teasing this audience with the Firm's growth plans, their attention will switch to what he has in mind from what has already been reported on. The negative press will end up as a temporary distraction, albeit a painful one. There has been no criminal wrongdoing, and any lapses in judgment have been dealt with internally. The Firm, though disappointed by the behavior of a few bad or unwise apples, will carry on with its fiduciary duty to investors and continue with its growth plans.

Privately, the Founder is furious, but he chooses to bury this emotion because he knows that what is valuable to the Firm is to move on without any more noise. He cannot talk about how distasteful he finds the matter. That would be inappropriate. His task is to reforge how the Firm's investors and the public will see these events, as part of a painful process the Firm is going through to "grow up" as a public corporation, as its rivals will have to do as well, to embrace and cultivate a better, more responsible culture. Then, to gain further ground, to nail the interview, he reveals *part* of the endgame:

We are in the tenth year of an economic upcycle, setting aside the shock of the pandemic. Interest rates are low, and our investors require yield to service their obligations. The credit markets are frothy; even high-yield bonds are now issued at an interest rate of only five percent and do not offer investors much protection if the investment goes wrong. There is a worldwide search for yield. We aim to maintain our discipline and buy assets that are highly likely to both return our investors' money and make a return on their money. If we do this, which I am confident we will, then by growing our platforms and franchise, we should manage over a trillion dollars of capital within the next decade—double the amount we manage today. And unlike vanilla firms that passively track the market, we will do better than the market. That is how we plan to expand from here, through consistent investment performance and through transparency of our mission like the kind I am talking about today. That is how our stock will soon be eligible for inclusion in the S&P 500 index.

With that final sentence, the penny drops. The Founder has thrown down the gauntlet to critics by being frank about the balance of power in the asset management industry. He came out fighting, but without looking like he was fighting. He was not defensive about the Firm's recent issues, and he knows that the bombshell of doubling assets under management to over a trillion dollars and joining the S&P 500 index is enough for the chatter to shift from the past to the future. He's pivoted the story.

The S&P 500 is one of the most important stock market indices in the world. Admission to the elite club of companies that form part of the index requires specific criteria to be met, including market capitalization size and the percentage of shares in the public's hands. Several trillion dollars in passive vehicles such as ETFs track the S&P 500 as a proxy for the large cap U.S. stock market. If the Firm's stock were part of the S&P 500, major passive fund managers would buy the stock automatically. In turn, this demand for the Firm's stock would likely support the stock price—and raise it in line with greater demand. So far, in the private equity industry, no other firm's stock has ever been listed on the S&P 500. The Firm could be the first, and this move could add to the impressive list of pioneering achievements that the Founder has led in the industry. And since he is a major stockholder in the Firm, this move would also increase his net worth—and that of all of the Firm's employees who are rewarded in stock as well as in cash.

It's also true that pension funds and other investors in private equity funds might end up gaining exposure to the Firm multiple times—through their fund commitments and, if they invest in passive funds like index-tracking funds and ETFs, through the Firm's stock as well. This may already be the case, but if the Firm's stock were to be included in the S&P 500, it would be much more so. A double-dip of retirees' trust and capital.

What is striking about the Founder's PR maneuvers here is that he did not react to the crisis. *He responded to it.* And he did it on his own terms and in his own interest. He did not behave, like so many public figures in business and politics, like nothing wrong had been done and there was nothing to reply to. He was not the corporate executive acting like he was coated in Teflon, determined that nothing would stick. His reply was to spell out in simple terms how the Firm and he would learn from the past and grow better despite what had happened. He succeeded in sounding *humble* when calmly laying out how the Firm would set aside the issues and *still* progress.

The Founder demonstrated the most elusive trait of big success in private equity over the long term: the paramount importance of temperament.

*   *   *

At that very moment, in Midtown Manhattan, a mid-level, early thirties private equity professional at the Firm is being interviewed by the seventy-something founder of one of the Firm's fiercest competitors. The rival firm is older and places particular value in its brand, as it has perhaps the most dignified name in the business. It does not negotiate as hard as the Firm does; it does not look to squeeze the last drop out of each set of economics. The pay is about twenty percent lower, but the young executive does not care. He does not feel that he fits into the more aggressive fabric of the Firm and wants a change. He can be as fierce a negotiator as the next guy, but he wants to develop his career in a less ruthless climate. Some of his college friends work at the competitor, and he wants to join them. The interview is the final round of an exhausting process, consisting of aptitude tests, a psychometric evaluation, and early morning and weekend video conference meetings organized in secret. The rival founder is not fond of the Firm, and the feeling is mutual. The competitors battle over deals, over investors' money, and, most bitterly, over retention of talent. And in reality, the rivalry is a battle between two billionaires, not just their companies.

The septuagenarian boss of the rival firm is immaculately dressed in a navy two-piece woolen suit, a crisp white shirt with a midnight blue silk tie and matching pocket square, and polished black loafers with tassels. Each item is bespoke, one of many in his collection. In fact, he owns a number of the attire manufacturers, because keeping niche family businesses alive is one of his hobbies. His blue eyes are deep with experience, and he asks the young man how he would describe the culture at the Firm. He is really asking about the Founder more than he is asking about the company that he competes with. And after hearing less than two sentences of the reply, he abruptly cuts the candidate off. He offers his take on the Firm, seeking to assess how the hire reacts. He does not hold back.

> They have no culture. No culture. I would not give them the time of day. Everyone knows they are good investors. But we are good too, and we achieve this with a culture of partnership, not a climate of fear and envy. We have built a firm with a great culture. We are not aggressive for the sake of being aggressive. I'm not scared of them, and neither is anyone else here. Until now, I have never hired from them, because sharp-elbowed people would not fit in here. What would you say to that?

It is a critical career moment for the recruit. It is not in his interest to agree or to disagree, but he must still have an opinion. He must show that his spine is made of steel and that he is smart enough to have a view that is at least insightful, but he cannot appear to be either a sycophant or a traitor. The wrong move can certainly end his career. And in this moment, he asks himself: *What would the Founder of the Firm say to that?* He summons the blood rushing through his head, speaks in a humble but firm whisper, and states the real reason that he wants to work for the old man's outfit: He wants to work for leaders who are *role models*.

The rival founder loves this answer. He walks the young man to the elevator himself, a sure sign of approval, and leaves little doubt about the success of the interview with a couple of positive signals.

"This was constructive. You are a competent guy," he says.

"I like you, despite where you work, and I trust you," he adds a moment later.

The young man walks across Fifth Avenue back to Park Avenue and considers a few stark contrasts between the competing firms. He has only a few minutes to himself to think. His make-believe dentist's appointment is over, and he must now return to his work before his absence is noticed. From the outside, the firms are different. Certainly, the optics clash. The Firm is housed in modern offices with standing desks and plain conference rooms. Partners skip wearing a tie. The look and feel is relaxed but serious. The competitor looks more like a traditional private bank in Europe. Silk ties, French cuff links, pocket squares. The partners look like wealthy diplomats, and the offices showcase modern art on the walls and chandeliers overhead. The rival thinks of itself as the figurehead for the private equity industry. Shouting is rare, and bullying is banned. The investment committee is a robust but civilized forum. Perhaps the Firm has the better investors, for it generates higher returns. The Firm can be an aggressive place to work. It is in the Founder's DNA to fight.

Both firms are excellent training grounds and provide rewarding careers. The recruit wants to jump ship because he does not feel that he fits the mold of the Firm, not because he is unhappy with the work. He asks himself why the rival founder was dismissive of the Firm and recalls that the competitor came off far worse in a recent battle between the two private equity firms over a distressed asset. The rival lost five hundred million dollars when one of its leveraged buyouts imploded, only to see the Firm pick up the pieces out of bankruptcy and go on to make a killing. Perhaps the old man is a bit jealous, although he knows there must be more to the rivalry that sits behind the scenes. But it is not his place or problem to get involved in a rich man's brawl.

What he does reflect on is how the rival founder's poker face cracked when he began discussing the Founder. The rival could not help presenting himself as a noble statesman, as the better citizen. The candidate has likely landed the role partly because he was able to flatter the old man; that would never have worked on the Founder. Getting the job was, if he was honest, easier than he had thought it would be.

After the offer is finalized, the young man resigns from the Firm and serves out his notice period. If the Founder is irritated that one of his finest young investors was poached, he does not show it. He remembers it, saves it for later.

The young man starts at the rival firm within three months and enjoys the more collegiate structure that he has joined, including the invaluable help and friendship of a female mentor a few years his senior. They work together closely, and she becomes a guide to his new environment. And he maintains his own temperament when it is announced, a few months later, that his mentor has been fired, and it becomes known that he is destined to be her replacement. He is promoted into the empty space that she was forced to vacate, and so begins his flourishing career. He is told that she lost her cool too often and did not fit in. He does not react. He responds, presenting himself as a paragon of stability, a contrast. Although he finds this approach to be distasteful, it gives him the best chance to succeed. He wonders . . . perhaps the rival firms are not so different after all?

The two sketches above are rooted in real experiences. What they illustrate about private equity is that even if emotions are running high and the stakes are visible and significant, whether defending a firm as its leader or navigating a dream job at a bitter rival, unlike so many other areas of business the most important decisions are often taken without emotion. The horizon of a private equity investment is not measured in minutes or days, like a liquid trade in stocks or bonds. Likewise a career; it takes decades and several major investments seen from entry to exit. This time horizon goes hand in hand with making judgments for the long run. For aspiring practitioners, this skill is perhaps the hardest to learn and the worst to get wrong.

The Founder's TV interview reply to the issues facing the Firm is only the start of what he had in mind. He plans to respond in careful steps, announcing some of them in advance and keeping the rest secret. The first stage is to let the markets and the media digest his words. The second will be to continue the response with a strategic initiative. He designs each move to gradually reveal how powerful and broad the blueprint for the Firm really is. It is already more than a private equity fund; it manages multiple investment strategies for private capital and is referred to as an alternative asset manager. But until now, it has been beyond the direct reach of ordinary citizens. Only institutional investors, such as pension funds and sovereign wealth funds, can invest. This will soon change.

After the Davos conference, the Founder travels onward to elite gatherings in California and Asia. Billionaires and other powerful public figures travel in Gulfstream private jets to attend these private forums to discuss the problems facing society and the economy and to explain how their businesses are helping as well as thriving through them. At these subsequent events, the

Founder makes similar comments to his statements at the World Economic Forum, and they are well received. It becomes clear in the next year that the Firm is likely to achieve the objectives he previewed in his CNBC interview. The stock soon does become part of the S&P 500. In verticals such as life sciences and insurance, colossal deals are struck in which the private equity or credit funds acquire an interest in large companies and provide capital for acquisitions. There is almost no end in sight. Assets under management climb by over fifty billion dollars every year. It is clear that private equity has become the Big Tech of the finance industry. Too important to fail. Too vital to stop. It is everywhere.

The masterstrokes of the Founder's next steps to grow the Firm are delivered without pomp or forewarning to the financial markets. The Firm acquires a midsize asset manager of mutual funds and passive funds that cater directly to retail investors, to mom-and-pop investors, and to other 401(k) savers. The unit offers old-fashioned "buy and hold" index trackers and ETFs, the kind of vehicles that sit on the opposite end of the money management spectrum from private equity. The Firm's share price is riding high, given a boost by inclusion into a major index, so the acquisition is paid for in stock. It looks like a smart bargain. The unit is acquired by the Firm itself, for the benefit of the Firm, not by the private equity fund or by the other private capital vehicles.

The first twelve months at the acquired unit bring a suite of measures often employed by private equity managers for a portfolio investment. The Firm upgrades the senior executives, trims excessive costs, and makes impactful client-facing hires. The Firm also makes calculated investments in technology, overhauling systems that will improve how management can analyze and run the operations. The business is rebranded to fit the corporate look and feel of the Firm.

The integration of the business goes well, but the financial markets seem to expect more—something more strategic to this move than the Founder has so far let on. The unit caters to retail investors, not pension funds, and working for individuals can mean less privacy and more regulation. The Firm is usually at pains to distinguish its work from that of such money managers. Little is said about the unit on the Firm's quarterly earnings calls, leaving its research analysts and rivals to play a guessing game. What is really happening?

The answer is that the Firm is learning. The Founder aims to offer private equity vehicles and the other investment strategies managed by the Firm directly to the public. He aims to go retail, ahead of his competitors, adding direct investments by 401(k) and other retail savers to the long list of ways that retirees can entrust their pension money to the Firm. His investment professionals are studying the unit, analyzing the flows of money, drafting ideas for new versions of the Firm's famous private equity, credit, real estate, and infrastructure funds that can be sold directly to retail investors. The vehicles will likely need to have greater diversification across investments than the private equity funds that invest the capital of retirement systems and other large investors. They will be regulated more strictly, and that is why Wall Street attorneys are working hard in the background to craft the documentation. Risk factors will be highlighted in bold and have boxes drawn around them for emphasis. The partners debate terms for these new products, such as how liquid they will be, how valuation updates will be provided to investors, and what type and level of fees will be charged. It won't be Two and Twenty. But the figure should be markedly more expensive than going to a good Main Street shop like Black-Rock. The funds should have premium brand value.

The plan is teased out to the financial markets over the next twelve months. The Firm's government affairs group in Washington and (somewhat more efficaciously) the Founder speak regularly to policymakers about the missed opportunity that is being forced upon retail investors under the current regulations. Surely, they argue, ordinary workers cannot just rely on Big Tech shares in their investment portfolios in the blind hope that they will continue to appreciate. They should diversify—and be allowed to buy stock in the Rolls-Royces of the finance industry too. Why not let the public access the products of private equity firms directly? Their collective lobbying efforts take time, but after a further year of due process and tweaks to the regulations, retail funds from the Firm are green-lighted for sale. These retail funds are handled by the Firm's acquired funds business, an investment that has been honed and improved—and has been preparing for this event.

As retail investors' money starts to pour in, attracted by the Firm's investment track record and brand, competitors play catch-up. In particular, the firm led by the immaculately dressed rival is left standing. By tapping into the enormous market for retail investors' money, the Founder has lit another one of the growth engines that is helping to double the Firm's assets under management. The Founder does not gloat, nor does he underplay his success. When he speaks about the Firm's progress in the media, how far it has come from the issues faced just a few years before, he is factual, pensive, and concise. He is grateful.

The Founder is also not obsessed with making money, at least not in a recognizable way. There are no celebrations of results as one might expect on the heady trading floors of an investment bank or a hedge fund. He works twelve hours a day, six days a week. He donates generously to a wide range of humanitarian and philanthropic causes, including museums and schools. He is driven by an insatiable thirst to succeed, and yet he is patient. His mentor often suggested that the right goal in private equity is to be "long-term greedy." The Founder's temperament allows him to execute his ideas to win and to create wealth over the long term.

In the next chapter, we move on from discussing the key attributes for successful investment professionals to succeed in private equity to an understanding of the key identified behaviors of those at the absolute top of the industry, the masters of private equity. We start with their need to win.

# CHAPTER EIGHT

# If You Don't Ask, You Don't Win

As a master of private equity, you must win.

There is no deal profit to be shared if you *almost* exit an investment successfully, or if you *nearly* make the project work. If you do not score a victory and generate the return sold to investors, there is no point to your job.

If you don't win, the retirement systems might as well invest passively in the stock and bond markets at a tiny fraction of your cost. The investors might as well establish their own units for direct investing into companies and finance them as if they were private equity firms, not passive investors in funds. You might as well go home. This is the brutal reality of working in private equity, and it is part of why the industry attracts and cultivates professional *risk-takers who need to win.*

They understand that success is binary; investors either receive the range of returns on capital they were expecting from private equity, or they do not. There is little pressure to invest for the sake of putting money to work, even when private equity firms are flush with cash. There is, however, constant pressure to deliver.

Success, defined as making money on deals, always comes first. The way that this success is executed takes account of other important factors, from helping enterprises grow to contributing to communities, but in the end, it is the moneymaking that counts the most. Success validates years of work on deals that might have started off badly or taken a while to pursue, confirms the necessity of painful business restructurings, and provides a clear answer to regulators and policymakers who might wish to pressure the industry into charging lower fees and paying higher taxes. When there is repeat success, over economic cycles, it is untenable to argue that the industry is not essential to retirees. Private equity's success is retirement systems' gain.

What success looks like in private equity is no secret. It involves buying well at reasonable prices. It requires partnering with management teams and independent non-executive directors. It involves transforming and improving the operations of target companies, which may involve making bolt-on acquisitions and executing organic growth initiatives. It involves financing and refinancing investments opportunistically when interest rates and other terms are compelling. It involves exiting well and creatively, in one step or in stages, in such a way that maximizes the blended sale price. It requires assembling a winning combination of most if not all of these deal elements together.

The billionaires at the top of the major firms in the industry, the masters of private equity, epitomize the culture of no-excuses success that is central to its existence and is even part of the profession's attraction for new recruits. These folks are built to win, through design and force of will. They understand that it is impossible to run away from big mistakes and that every investor is as good as their deal track record—without airbrushing out the mishaps. They acknowledge the public responsibility that flows from their judgment, and they would be the last people to either fake success or disown failure. They accept that the code of taking ownership applies to everyone working in private equity. They appreciate and encourage that the playing field in private equity is level and that intelligence and hard work bring more success to an established franchise with an investment track record.

They emphasize to colleagues that when things go wrong, there is nowhere to hide and no point in trying to hide. Transparency is key. They keep moving; they are always working the angles and cannot bear to lose a deal—unless they are convinced that other bidders are making a mistake by winning that will come back to bite them. And we expect them to win, given the incentive provided by Two and Twenty and how much is at stake for them personally. They would be the first in the investment committee to expose weakness in an investment thesis and would not sugarcoat the bitter medicine needed to get a wayward deal back on track. The founders of the major private equity firms are not just figureheads. They are the ones bureaucrats in governments and at central banks often call when they want to understand the shape of the economy and some of its systemic risks. They tell a situation like it really is.

This culture cascades through private equity firms from top to bottom. The first time a freshly minted recruit sees a billionaire founder agonize over the key details of a deal, rather than only focus on the big picture from thirty thousand feet, they know the bar is set high—but achievably high—at every level of the organization. In briefings between juniors and mid-level professionals, every conceivable angle of an investment's analysis is explored, and each draft of investment committee materials is pored over. The deal partner will have personal input into the financial model, and it is leadership, not ego, that they are putting into the team effort by doing this. The overriding questions for the team are: How can we do right by our investors, and how can we make money for them and our firm? With the territory comes an intense spotlight on performance, on micro decisions made each week, on working a triple shift to optimize each move of the chessboard.

This culture—this attitude—promotes a trail of personal hunger trickling down from the Gulfstream private jets to the juniors' bullpens. It is ingrained competition. Deal team members will ask each other whether a decision they plan to have management at a target company make is "smart," meaning: *Will it enhance the likelihood of compelling returns in line with the investment committee memo or better?* Young associates soon learn that having technical skill is not enough; it might have helped them get through the door, but their judgment will be assessed on whether and how the investment makes money—or might lose it. Using the autonomy that they are given in private equity to shape investments with management teams, they will do everything they can to maximize the chances of success.

Negotiation is central to this design. Iterative, constant, and relentless negotiation. The deal team members will ask themselves on each material point in the formulation of a business strategy or its execution: *Is this good enough? Can it be done better?* Call it haggling or hustling, the quest for improvement never stops. It is driven by the unyielding desire of each investment professional to optimize, whether that means driving a harder settlement on financing or beating the Firm's rivals to buying the right company at the right price. Deal teams are ready to negotiate for as long as it takes before the point of walking away, of no return, right up to that edge where private equity gets itself a great deal. The ethos handed down from the top is that you are more likely to find a smart bargain if you know how to bargain well.

"Maybe it's not a lot of money for you, but twenty million dollars is a lot for our investors. We should fight for it and strike a better outcome."

The Founder's observation draws raucous laughs and applause as he gently reprimands a young partner on a two-billion-dollar deal that involves a billion dollars of cash from the Firm's private equity fund. The newly promoted partner smiles nervously; he knows that the Founder is right. The investment is large, and so is the responsibility that comes with it, for every cent, and that is why his task should be to push the handful of Wall Street banks he is liaising with to accept a lower fee for their financing work. Exhausted, toiling around the clock, he had the audacity and naïveté to suggest that the Firm should accept the fees proposed by the banks, because they were tantamount to a rounding error.

The project is complex. Their target, PetCare Corporation, is a large retail chain specializing in food and grooming products for pets, with operations across the United States and in six international markets. Founded as a small company in California, PetCare grew in only four years to achieve this platform and is one of the darlings of the NASDAQ stock exchange. The company was the first of its kind and scale, introducing innovations like telemedicine for pets and the idea of pet food endorsed by celebrity chefs. But, unexpectedly, the company is on the ropes.

A series of pet food health scares and quality problems with pet clothing were met with an underwhelming response from the proud CEO who founded the business. The board of directors replaced him with a new CEO who was even worse, as he failed to fix the issues and then muddied the strategy with a vanity acquisition in the pet insurance sector that he was too distracted to oversee. The company is a mess, and, sensing blood in the water, competitors have slashed prices to take market share and rub the shine off the industry leader.

One of the Firm's private equity rivals controls the business, having bought it from the venture capitalists in Palo Alto who financed the start-up of PetCare in an auction run by Wall Street banks—in which the Firm was decisively outbid. Post-acquisition, as each step of the business plan to grow nationally and overseas was executed, the rival added incremental leverage to the company's books before filing for an IPO, knowing that the frothy equity markets would likely forgive a high level of buyout debt in a turbocharged growth stock. But now, with PetCare's fortunes on the decline, the private equity firm is looking for a way to cash out, if not entirely then at least to reduce its billion dollars of remaining exposure.

The buyout bonds and loans secured on the company have crashed in price and are trading at a thirty percent discount to their original value—and are due to be repaid at this higher value. With incoming cash flow under rising pressure, the business needs to refinance, and lenders are reluctant to upsize the vital lines of credit required for working capital. It's like PetCare went from Most Valuable Player to outcast in no time at all. Within six months, the company will likely face a credit crunch that could prove to be terminal for the business.

Enter the Firm. Losing out on the auction for PetCare was a blow for the young partner who led the project; it was his first taste of failure in his new senior role. In hindsight, perhaps losing out was a blessing. He now has the chance to take hold of the company at a lower valuation than it was sold for. Sometimes a canny operator—or, at least, an operator who looks canny in retrospect—wins by not paying the highest price. Now, the new partner may have the chance to pick up the business for a fraction of its fundamental value.

What he proposes to the private equity owner of PetCare is for the Firm to step into the worn-out shoes of the company's lenders, consolidate the existing debt into a loan facility from the private equity funds of the Firm, and keep this debt private and untraded, out of the markets' spotlight. The Firm will not acquire the target outright—it will acquire the debt outstanding from the target and become the new lender to the target. The loan facility will be sizable enough to house spare liquidity, should the company need it for working capital or emergencies. With the refinancing solved in this way, the private equity owner will be free to resume focusing on PetCare's growth trajectory, paving the way for a more profitable exit down the line when the issues in the business are resolved.

The young partner pitches his plan to the target's board as a win-win situation: PetCare gets breathing space for repairs and the Firm invests in a credit that it likes.

"We're here to help." His opening line.

In truth, the young partner has a chance through this structure to move in for the kill, and the rival knows it. In fact, he is eager to snare this prize asset from a rival, and his offer of a loan, even for a billion dollars, is no olive branch. He has waited patiently, and objectively, to see if the company he lost out on in an auction will face the kind of hairy situation that the Firm is well positioned to take advantage of as an expert in complex investments. This could be a lucrative big-ticket trade.

PetCare may not have much of a choice other than to accept the young partner's proposal. The private equity owner has too much exposure to this investment to double down; its fund is too concentrated to allocate more cash to PetCare. The Firm's offer can be delivered quickly, it is reliable, and it is a one-shot solution. And ironically, rather than making PetCare look desperate, the markets will likely regard the debt consolidation and fresh liquidity as a vote of confidence from a respected competitor. To outsiders, it will almost look as if the rivals are working together toward a common goal.

Of course, this is not exactly the case. The Firm is a lender *with an agenda.* PetCare will now have one large and powerful creditor that happens to be its owner's competitor. Information barriers will be respected, of course. But the clear fact is that were the company to slip up further, the business would be on the hook to a rival where the investment professionals personally feel the need to win, to make the most of the situation, and to optimize the return for their investors—not just to settle for an acceptable outcome. This is evident in the terms of the new debt for PetCare, which features a higher interest rate, strict covenants, and far less wiggle room to file for bankruptcy and saddle the Firm with a loss.

In fact, if things do not pick up, it would not be too hard for the Firm to call time on the new debt and ask to be repaid immediately. Litigation might ensue, but the Firm would be in a commanding position. The young partner *might* have suggested definitively to the investment committee that the Firm would be lucky to own PetCare under these circumstances, but this information is not likely to air during a restructuring. The Firm would look like any other lender. Except that this lender is not a Wall Street bank or a credit fund. It is part of a private equity firm with the experience and desire to own and manage businesses for the benefit of its investors. Borrow from a bank, and you do not normally expect the folks that you are dealing with to be fine with the idea of taking over. They're interested in debt repayment, with repossession as a last resort they do not welcome.

What the situation also highlights is the asymmetry of terms between when the Firm acts as a lender, offering credit for companies to grow and financing buyouts for rivals, and when the Firm acts as a borrower, raising debt for its private equity investments.

When financing its own buyouts, the Firm drives a hard but transparent bargain for the weakest package of creditor protections for lenders—including debt covenants and other restrictions. Some of these restrictions might, for example, limit the ability of the private equity fund to pile on more debt without permission from existing lenders. Or they might stop valuable assets from being taken out of the package of security that lenders have in case things go wrong, which would mean they cannot be taken over by creditors. Or they might be restrictive when it comes to paying out dividends to the private equity fund. Most likely, it will be a combination of such protections in some form that creditors would look for. It's a zero-sum game: The weaker the creditor protections are, the stronger the position of the Firm on behalf of its investors in the private equity fund. It's in these investors' interest for the Firm to negotiate this way, because if something were to go wrong with the deal, it is in their interest to be in the best position possible vis-à-vis creditors.

Most credit investors reluctantly accept this imbalance of power because they are thirsty for yield in a macro environment where central banks have kept interest rates low to support the economy. When credit investors compete with each other to buy this debt the Firm is raising for its private equity investments, it's often a race to the bottom on terms—an auction to the highest bidder who is willing to take the most risk.

In contrast, when financing competitors' deals, the exact

opposite is true. Here, the Firm will insist on the strongest package of protections possible as well as other terms, such as an option to be part of the equity ownership in some manner, in some cases. After all, the Firm is not a passive participant. The micro steps of negotiating these points for the Firm are where the value will lie, and that is why this takes investment professionals who need to win. This is what is in the interest of the Firm's investors who have put money into the Firm's funds that will hold this debt. The tables are turned because the investors are now on the other side of the deal.

The Firm has the power to act in this way, to have different objectives and one might say different standards for creditor protections and other terms, including pricing and participation in the equity, when it lends versus when it borrows. A creditor can expect a tough conversation with the Firm if seeking to accelerate or enforce its protections against a portfolio company it has lent to. Conversely, a borrower breaches a creditor protection owed to the Firm when it lends out, such as in a debt covenant, at its peril. You do not want to be in the position where the fate of your business is now in the hands of private equity that has lent to you. The Firm is in this enviable position because of its expertise and because it plays in both the borrower and the creditor sandboxes at tremendous scale. And the folks who run the Firm run it all.

The young partner is excited about the deal because the situation does not call for the type of plain vanilla lending where it would be difficult to negotiate hard as a creditor. The credit markets are so frothy that "ordinary" lending would end up being executed at unfavorable terms, at a very low interest rate and with weak creditor protections. That is the kind of deal he would prefer to decline. Instead, he is keen to engage in this situation because it is not an ordinary one. He can lend to PetCare at scale in a complex situation. The terms of this specialized lending are more favorable, and as a lender, he won't even mind very much if he has the chance to take the target over. In fact, you might say he has something of an incentive to do just that if the chance were to emerge.

Ordinary lenders are not interested in continuing to support PetCare, and in fact they are privately relieved to be cashed out. And so, the transaction presents the chance for the Firm to ask for more in discussions, opaquely at some junctures and directly at others, time and time again. To keep going back with one-sided additions to the terms that are beneficial for the Firm and its investors. After all, without the credit investment by the Firm's fund, PetCare would likely face bankruptcy, jeopardizing jobs and communities. The investment gives the company a second chance.

The young partner earns the respect of his peers by delivering an asymmetric risk/reward—limiting downside if the company's performance worsens and capturing some of the upside if the business improves. If PetCare does well, then along with hefty interest payments and repayment of the debt, the Firm will be granted a share of the equity, even though it did not pay for any of the equity in the first place. PetCare's success will then be part of the Firm's success, part of its own track record. The young partner negotiates the details of financing agreements night and day to achieve this goal, revealing an inner desire and requirement to get the better of every single material dialogue with his counterparties. He weaponizes the debt documentation where necessary to protect the Firm's investors.

The Founder's instruction to pay lower financing fees to the existing lenders being cashed out has provided the chance for the young partner to sharpen his knife on a few terms that are still in the mix. In the final hour, the young partner decides to add a two-million-dollar financing fee on top, this time payable to the Firm, as a one-time transaction fee for its work on the deal. "For the good guys," they joke.

That the Firm's competitor is fast-growing, successful, and an employer of choice on campuses and at investment banks adds irony to its predicament. When PetCare was auctioned and the Founder learned that the young partner had lost out to a higher bidder, he remarked, "Don't worry. The competition in the buyout space is weak."

The Founder was confident that for PetCare's board to pick a rival's offer despite the Firm's connections and market presence, the price would have to be crazy—too good to refuse. Similarly, when discussing in the investment committee where the young partner had gotten to in the negotiations and how much of the effort going forward to monitor and help the business would now be squarely on the Firm's shoulders, rather than the current private equity owner, the Founder remarked, "The good news is, we are the ones doing all the work."

This satisfaction with the burden of taking the lion's share of the workload from an existing owner, and the spoils that come with it, remind the Founder of an anecdote that he thinks is apt to share with the young partner and his deal team.

It was seven years ago, and the Founder was leading the buyout of a publicly listed casino operator. The target was a sleepy company, resting on its laurels, and had plenty of potential to improve profitability by cutting out fat, focusing on fewer business lines, and making small, tuck-in acquisitions. Due diligence was progressing well, until loose words about the project from a Wall Street financing bank leaked to the media. All hell broke loose.

An exclusive, bilateral discussion blew open to a formal auction. Every major private equity firm was desperate to run a slide rule over the business, to check if they should bid for the company and to understand what promise the Firm saw in the target. Deal teams from competing firms rotated in and out of the casino operator's headquarters in Nevada like the ball on a roulette wheel. The chair of the business felt like a croupier, managing a high-stakes game with his management team's and employees' careers at stake. As well as his own.

"It's just external noise," the Founder reassured his colleagues when they expressed grave concern that one of the new bidders had matched the Firm's offer for the business, with the equity check now likely to be split between the two rivals. It didn't matter to the Founder that the Firm and its competitor were forced to team up on the deal, to persuade public shareholders that there really was no better price out there for the target and to avoid a bidding war. It wasn't important that the rivals did not like each other and that the relationship would be harsh during the term of the investment. What mattered was that the Founder saw that the Firm was likely to continue to do and lead most of the work, drive the target, and make the investment a success. The rest was noise, irrelevant to the overriding goal to succeed, to win. It would have been better if the two private equity firms had been natural partners, likely to cooperate, but they were not. What mattered was that the Firm didn't care if it dragged a co-investor along for the ride. It would achieve its objective regardless.

The same ethos is alive with today's deal. The Founder has so much faith in the culture of his organization that he is confident that if anyone can make money out of the investment, his folks can. Because they work harder, and they work smarter. Because they will seek to maximize every material part of the investment, relenting only when there is little benefit to continuing to push further. When settling becomes *smarter* than negotiating.

The young partner's masterstroke has been to stay engaged in the situation long after losing the public auction. He has marshaled the Firm's resources to create a sound credit investment and perhaps an option to control the company on attractive terms.

By consolidating the debt, the money that the Firm's investors have put in is senior to and safer than the rival's equity in the company. The "attachment point" is higher up the stack of money financing the business; they are more likely to get paid back if PetCare falls off the edge. And unlike a bank without a private equity team standing by, the Firm has a private equity franchise that would love to get hold of the company if the circumstances arise.

The young partner will self-generate the pressure he will feel during the life of the investment, to keep moving and stay on the edge, to monitor carefully whether there is a chance to upsize the debt being provided—say, to finance growth if the company is doing well—and to consider next steps. He is not surrounded by sharks, of course, but he appreciates that if he doesn't have the need to win, someone else will—either the colleagues who might be drafted in to help him or counterparties at the rival private equity firm. This is part of why he fuels his own momentum.

He will not care much for taking credit in public about lending to a competitor's ailing investment. His satisfaction, and his reward, will come from the result on PetCare, not boasting about it.

And although thousands of hours of work have already been invested into achieving this situation for the Firm, the work needed to generate a handsome return for the retirement systems and other investors putting up the money and paying Two and Twenty has only just started. If PetCare's performance worsens, it will need to be restructured or reborn or stripped apart. If it does well, the business and the Firm need to discuss the equity share promised as part of the negotiation. The heavy lifting starts here.

It is important to understand that investment professionals like the young partner in our sketch are not outliers. He is a product of training, of a system, of an industry. He will have innate drive, because without it there is no chance that he will survive. But the ecosystem of private equity has undoubtedly shaped him, incentivized him, propelled him. Each of the major firms is staffed with its share of alpha types, some more so than others, and there is a little alpha in everyone who works as an investment professional in the industry. It is not about ego; it is about an unyielding requirement to succeed because of their personalities and the economics involved. Whether PetCare ultimately sails through its problems or is sold to WalMart or Amazon or someone else, the young partner will help ensure that the retirees keep getting their checks.

In this chapter, we have focused on the need for a winning mentality at the heart of private equity and how it drives good outcomes for fund investors. In the next, we elaborate how a deeply competitive spirit drives actions and behavior. Private equity folks have multiple tools at their disposal that showcase this attribute, one of them being the ability to reengineer a target with a mediocre outlook to one that will make an excellent investment.

# CHAPTER NINE

# How to Make More

"Sugar, fat, and salt. We sell three magic ingredients."

The founder and CEO of Charlie's Cookies is unrepentant. The company he founded is an American icon, a household name that has fueled hardworking families with sweet baked goods for over forty years. His employees serve fresh baked chocolate chip, walnut, and oat raisin sweet wonders at one hundred stores in the company's franchise network and in three hundred more locations in cities around the world. In the past, the CEO has proudly rebuffed takeover offers that would have made him a billionaire, without regard to whether they came from private equity firms or rival chains. For decades, the CEO has relied on his innate sense of what his customers want and has been happy to provide it. When he founded the company in 1982, a single six-hundred-calorie cookie cost just 50 cents, and now it's $2.99—still a bargain. His brand is the envy of the global market for baked treats.

But times are changing. The cookie purveyor, now seventy-five years old, no longer has the energy to wake up at five o'clock in the morning and call a dozen of his bakeries from a random list to check how the first batch of cookies is coming along. He does not have the stamina to vet each new corporate employee or quiz each supplier of Belgian chocolate or Australian macadamia nuts or Mexican vanilla. He cannot wrap his head around the idea of selling online or home delivery or contemplate any of the blockbuster financing trades or acquisitions that excite the Wall Street bankers who make their quarterly pilgrimage from their skyscrapers to his mansion in upstate New York. The CEO feels spent. And what eats away at him the most is the painful reality that none of his four children or his eleven grandchildren have shown the remotest interest in taking over the reins of the business.

Charlie's faces an uncertain future. It is 2016, and an unstoppable trend toward cleaner, greener eating is taking its toll on revenues. The customer base has started to look like a melting ice cube, and inventories seem to fatten further by the month. With cash flow and profits stagnating, despite a hardcore base of loyalists, the junk bonds that financed a recent refit of the company's stores and its overseas footprint now look as appealing to credit investors as the junk food that the company's ovens pump out look to health-conscious consumers. The business needs to cut costs, but the old man is loath to slash jobs in the same local communities that made him so successful. He needs working capital, and he needs money to buy precious time, to refocus Charlie's, to save his life's work. That is why he has come to the Firm. He now sits in its boardroom, where the soaring views stretch out over Park Avenue. The CEO is trying to persuade the deal partner in the private equity group and his colleague in the credit group that they would be fortunate to be a part of the company's future and benefit from its storied past. The two seasoned dealmakers at the Firm are looking at specific angles for a potential investment into Charlie's. They might end up combining their ideas, working together, or going with either of their solutions—or walking away. The CEO has to sell the story, and the Firm has to be willing to buy into that story, one way or another.

Unbeknownst to the CEO, however, a turf war is brewing. The deal partner from the private equity group respects but is uncomfortable with the presence of his credit fund partner in the meeting. He feels the project should be an investment for his fund alone. The credit specialist feels likewise. Each one thinks that putting money into Charlie's to fix what does not work and improve what does is the way forward. But neither wants the other to be in charge of the deal.

Each partner is sitting on tens of millions of dollars' worth of the Firm's stock and will benefit from dividends resulting from the deal no matter which pocket of capital—private equity or credit—invests in the company. Neither likes the idea of the other being seen as the better one to lead the investment. They are rivals and they are colleagues. They each want the other one to succeed, but not as much as they want themselves to succeed. This competitive dynamic is found in many areas of the finance industry, but in private equity, given the scale of compensation and the autonomy commanded by senior investment professionals, it can be acute.

Finally, the Founder enters the room, immediately gesturing for everyone present to retake their seats when they stand up abruptly, showing respect and maybe a little fear. It was the Founder's idea to have the CEO meet both groups. The Founder believes that a little internal competition can be healthy—a way to help the Firm get to the right answer. He believes it is the correct path to putting investors' money to work. He is aware of, and does not mind, the modest discomfort that each of his two lieutenants feels. The two warriors will work together to drill the CEO, but they will also try to outdo each other, to persuade the CEO that only their own group has the right concept to lead the project to success—without looking as if the Firm has different pockets of capital that can sometimes compete to do a particular deal. They have to show strong unity, while at the same time carefully vocalizing the strengths of their own stalls. It's a well-worn balancing act, and one that to the untrained eye isn't too visible. The CEO will see a firm brimming with ideas, fired up in its imagination of how it can help, with two helpful partners having a healthy and open discussion with him—as if he's already part of their investment portfolio. It will look good, it will be genuine, and it will be helpful.

The Founder's immediate concern is to steer the business away from the Firm's rivals. The CEO is selling Charlie's story to the Firm, but the Founder must also persuade the CEO that the Firm is his best option, more so than rival private equity firms. And so the Founder beckons the old man to sit next to him at the head of the boardroom, and the two men hold a private chat that is almost inaudible amid the hum of the expensive air-conditioning flowing through the room. The Founder tells the CEO that he sympathizes with his situation and with the decision that has to be made about whom to trust among the major private equity firms and Wall Street banks. The Founder encourages him to contemplate not only where he has come from and what he has achieved but also where he is going and where Charlie's could end up without the Founder's help—and more important, without the Founder's friendship and connections. The company is in trouble, both men know it, and the CEO must prioritize survival over pride and trust the kind of partners that can get him out of his mess, even if it costs him a little independence. He needs investors who will both think and fight relentlessly, for him and for the sake of the consumers who adore the trans fats–laden goodies that the business churns out. Investors who will get Charlie's back into the black.

As if to take the old man into his confidence, the Founder recounts a war story, one of hundreds in his arsenal. He keeps it brief, but laces the yarn with plenty of brand names, as if to suggest that the CEO is being let in on a sensitive secret. The tale concerns a profitable business called Virginia Papers, a small division of a powerful but low-profile industrial conglomerate. Virginia is one of the top five makers of specialized paper coverings for cigarettes and cigars. Unknown to most, it is partly owned by the Firm's private equity fund. It all started two decades ago, the Founder explains, when the current climate for tobacco regulation started to take hold. Advertising was banned or highly restricted in developed markets, and in developing economies, health concerns were starting to impact sales. Virginia's parent, in the middle of a costly and complex acquisition of a small rival, was facing stiff opposition against the deal from activist hedge funds and skeptical public shareholders. The Founder ran his own deals then, and as he was friendly with the conglomerate's chairman, he offered to help out in a confidential capacity.

The Firm helped to finance the acquisition with its credit funds, and it sought to avoid attracting publicity, as this would draw undue attention to the tobacco products sector. In return, Virginia's parent sold a minority stake in the cigarette paper maker to the Firm's private equity fund. The money influx from this investment provided the group with useful cash at a time when the economic cycle was in a trough. The investment was structured as a debt instrument, but with certain voting rights added on top—a hybrid. As the deal was relatively small, it was not, in the grand scheme of things, material for the Firm or its funds. The Founder was true to his word and has neither gloated over nor revealed the existence of the investment—until this point. Now, however, the Founder knows that the story of this investment can help secure a new, not dissimilar deal, in a sector that is also health-sensitive. A sector that relies on selling sugar, fat, and salt—openly, with indulgence as an irresistible part of the allure.

In deploying the anecdote now, the Founder has sought to build trust, demonstrate discretion, and illustrate his pragmatic side. And he knows how to tell a story: The Founder's tone is blunt, gentle, and entirely convincing. He goes on to explain to the CEO that every relevant company in the Firm's portfolio will be drafted to assist Charlie's—businesses ranging from food additives to plastic packaging to logistics to hospitality and retail. They will look at every cell in the Excel spreadsheets that map the finances and prospects of the enterprise. The Firm's professionals will cross-check the assumptions made by Charlie's management and point to potential pitfalls before they happen. The CEO's success will be the Firm's success, and vice versa. The Founder ends by underscoring what is at stake for the CEO personally—not only his life's work and reputation but the chance to create a philanthropic legacy. Perhaps, the Founder suggests, that could be a cause his family can be proud of, even if they are not interested in the high-calorie snacks he has peddled for decades. All the CEO must do is swallow a bit of pride and accept an inevitable future, rather than dwelling on past glory. The offer is a temptation that the old man cannot refuse.

"Ask yourself where the puck is *going*, not where it sits. You know the right answer."

The Founder's final words echo in the CEO's mind on his

way home. His decision is made. He will work with the Firm to arrest the company's bleeding and will relay his thoughts in an email to the two partners later that evening. The Firm is clearly sold on the idea of investing in Charlie's, and he has decided to let the Firm in the door.

Meanwhile, at the Firm, the same two partners are gathered in the Founder's office to debrief. The room is smaller than outsiders might guess. It is dominated by a large "Resolute"-style presidential desk in the center and a reclinable leather armchair behind it. The leather's shade of green is precisely that found on dollar bills—a small favor from the treasury secretary when the Firm was established. The office has no windows, despite being on the best floor of one of the most expensive skyscrapers in Manhattan, with Central Park visible in the distance. The walls are bare, made of the same stained oak as the desk and the floors. It is more of a den than a room, and the partners are made to stand, because there are no chairs for visitors. There are no memos or presentations, no laptops or desktop computers. There is no phone in the office either. The only inputs here are people and their arguments. Every person is on their own. Their success or failure comes from what is said.

The three men know a hot deal is in the works. It is inevitable that the CEO will call the Firm to discuss terms for an exclusive period during which the Firm and the company will examine what type of investment makes sense: a buyout, a financing, or some other combination of ideas from the private equity and credit groups. The Founder's charm and wisdom will tip the scales in the Firm's favor. The partners know that they must work together to come up with dispassionate and detailed analyses of Charlie's from all angles—financial, strategic, and political—to present to the Founder, for him to decide in the best interests of the Firm and its investors. Their presence at the meeting with the CEO and his management team was as much to tee up this internal competition as it was to nullify external competition from the Firm's rivals.

Whether the CEO can sense it or not, the two Firm partners know that they will likely have to rip Charlie's apart to save it—and to make a success of the money they want to put to work. They are motivated by a drive born of competition and winning. They will force changes in the business if they are not forthcoming—always with respect, but without hesitation. The old man will be left on the side of the road if he is not on board. It will be their personal objective as much as their professional goal to win. The drive to make Charlie's succeed will be a controlled obsession: finely measured, with an acute self-awareness.

And so the two partners get on with the job, scrutinizing the potential investment in greater detail in preparation for signing a deal. In the weeks that follow, the pair makes a formidable double act, reviewing and questioning every line item of the business and every number in the company's spreadsheets. They scrutinize each aspect of every product: provenance of ingredients, nutrition (what there is of it), the baking network and process, gaps in the sweet treats market, and so on. They consider how to optimize peak selling slots during the week and on the weekends. They focus on an online offering and home delivery. They tackle head-on the uncomfortable questions about obesity and associated diseases that the old man was in the habit of brushing away. They cut open sacred cows, including the special formula for cookies at the heart of the brand.

The duo is content as they near the end of their top-to-bottom examination, for they know there is a lot of money to be made. Charlie's is, as the private equity industry might put it, "a terrific opportunity for value creation." The partners refresh the company's business plan, toying with operational changes that are likely to work. New chemicals are tested that enhance flavor and allow for less sugar and butter in the mix for each cookie. They also last longer, meaning that together with preservatives the shelf life will be given an overdue boost. Customers will be able to enjoy the sweet treats for up to ninety days after manufacture, rather than watch them go stale after only a month. With production revamped, stores will no longer need to bake onsite, finally making way for centralized bakeries and a distribution network that supplies cookies when needed. The shops will become marketing fronts, points of client engagement, rather than little bakeries. A modern website will make instant ordering easy and assuage feelings of disappointment when the products run out. Charlie's will always have cookies to buy, all year round, only a few clicks away.

As part of the changes, the CEO is persuaded to introduce healthier product lines using butter alternatives like coconut and olive oils, and sugar alternatives like chopped dates and figs. The company's longtime clientele may not take a shine to them, but the young might. Adding protein, fiber, and vitamins could even make the cookies a meal replacement, if they are appropriately renamed and branded, perhaps with a few key celebrity endorsements. A team of consultants helps the partners consider whether collaborating with a weight-loss franchise is a step too far or an enlightened concept. Before long, the company is preparing to produce high-protein bars, oatmeal bakes, fiber cookies, and vitamin bites. The deal team and management decide that all products will be reduced in size by ten percent, saving costs as well as marketing a healthier cookie.

The two partners also realize that Charlie's capital structure needs their attention. The company issued high-yield bonds after a heavy sales pitch from Wall Street banks but did not really understand the risks or how to negotiate the documents in its favor. Credit investors could block valuable assets like the brand and intellectual property from being stripped out of the borrowing group and sold off or mortgaged again to raise debt in an emergency. The impact of deteriorating credit ratings on the business was lost on the CEO, which was somewhat understandable given that he had never borrowed a dime in his personal life. The family home was bought in cash, funded by decades of savings. Working capital was managed using cash in the attic. The partners devise a plan to refinance the existing debt when the operating changes they are discussing with the CEO result in stronger financial performance.

The Firm's playbook for improving the way Charlie's is run meets the CEO's approval, and the Firm strikes a deal that involves both the private equity group and the credit group. The private equity fund purchases a controlling stake in the business, the junk bonds are repurchased and refinanced with debt on better terms, and a new cash line from a revolving credit facility is organized. The plan works, and the partners are pleased with the results. The company is made to be slimmer and fitter, and its capital structure is now being managed more effectively. It's a sharper and leaner Charlie's at every level. Both partners join the board of the company. They will continue to work together and occasionally try to outdo each other. With costs slimmed, cash flow fattened, and the cookie range expanded, the Firm has created a winner. Paid influencers manage to make the retro brand seem cool for a new generation of consumers, and cameo videos with Hollywood types go viral.

The net result of these initiatives, plus customary matters such as upgrading mid-level members of the management team, is a projected tripling of profits and a robust growth rate for the next five years. At the height of its new fame, Charlie's is sold to an Asian multinational foods group keen to diversify overseas and to control the fast-growing sweet treats market at home—at a high price beyond the Firm's expectations.

Charlie's CEO, the Firm and its investors, and the new Asian owner each get what they wanted: the rejuvenation of a historic franchise to glory and growth, a pile of philanthropy capital for the old man's legacy, and exceptional returns for the Firm and its investors. These investors make over *five times* their money. These are the kinds of returns that keep retirement systems coming back for more. Millions of workers across America, Europe, and Asia eat Charlie's products, and most of them have no idea that the Firm's investment in and work with the company behind these treats has helped make their pensions more secure. In a way, these retirees of tomorrow are in the cookie business.

The Firm makes Two and Twenty on the investment, along with a few million dollars of transaction fees. When you add it all up, each dollar from the Firm's investors has turned into five dollars, of which one dollar is taken by the Firm as carried interest and other costs borne by the Firm's funds—and the other four dollars are returned to the investors. The Firm and its partners put up a fraction of the money, two percent in this deal, but overwhelmingly, it is their investors' money that was at risk.

It is important to emphasize the time frame of a private equity or credit investment. In the vast majority of cases, such as in our sketch, it is not a long-term strategic move meant to last for generations. There is no empire building or irreversible bet on the future. Neither is it high-frequency trading, squeezing profits out of moment-to-moment transactions. Rather, it is a medium-term allocation of investors' money, whether structured as the acquisition of part or all of a company or business or the provision or purchase of credit. It must be sold at some point. It is temporary.

What is also true is that this private capital often takes a huge risk to support a growing or struggling enterprise precisely when other sources of money do not want to help. In our sketch, the Firm takes an enormous risk (with its investors' capital) to turn Charlie's fortunes around, at short notice, shoring up employment for thousands and giving a historic brand a new lease on life, at a time when the threat of bankruptcy was genuine. In real life, there are thousands of examples like this one every year, where private capital examines the risk/return trade-off for enterprises that might be on their knees and have nowhere else to go. Public markets may not contribute a dime. Governments may turn a blind eye. Nobody else might care, partly because traditional sources of capital prefer safer, less complex bets.

When others flee, private equity steps in—and steps up. Through this lens, making Two and Twenty (or some variation thereof) doesn't seem so outsize a reward. Perhaps taking risks others avoid, sorting complexity into order, and having the vision to see what others do not see are understandable reasons to richly reward those who consistently generate solid returns.

Let's explore this reward-for-results dynamic a little further. To achieve the results private equity delivers, the deal professionals get involved actively, directly. They do the heavy lifting on each investment. Imagine a private equity investment as something like buying a home to fix up and sell after a few years.

To show the next buyer that the home has value worth paying for, you must ensure the improvements are significant. A lick of paint and a flower display when buyers are visiting will not be enough. So you consider adding a basement, converting the loft, moving walls and floor levels to optimize space and layout, installing a new kitchen and bathrooms. Now add a layer of risk. What if the house you bought was in an unproven area, and you are betting on a train station that is under construction? Your investment hinges on the neighborhood becoming the next chic place to live. If you have done your research, it can be an educated gamble. If you have not done your homework, it could be a disaster. A mortgage finances the majority of the purchase price, whether you rent the property or live there, and if you do not service your regular payments, you could lose the keys to the property. The bank takes security on the bricks and mortar for the debt it lends to acquire the place and gives you cash for the capital expenditure on top. As the creditor, the bank is first in line to be repaid if the investment goes badly wrong.

So far, I've painted a familiar picture. Now let's deepen the analogy to fit private equity. What if the money invested does not come from you, but from investors, because the scale of the project is large and complex? What if to figure out the best spots to buy property (good location, structural integrity and safety, proximity to schools and hospitals, outdoor space, and essential stores), you need data and contacts that are hard to come by? What if you need a team of heavyweight advisors to help execute what you want to change about the asset? What if, as you near the exit, you learn that finding a buyer is hard? Perhaps when you consider these points you decide to hire an asset manager to find and execute the deal for you. What if the asset manager can handle all these matters and has the time, resources, and experience to do a good job of it? And what if the asset manager can negotiate so well with creditors that they can avoid bankruptcy and keep ownership of the home, if needed, even during hard times? What if they are proven winners in trading not just homes but other types of property too, from office buildings to sports venues?

When you start to grasp the range of expertise the masters of private equity must bring to dealmaking, the compensation rates begin to come into focus. It's a premium service at a premium rate. We can also start to build a picture of how the top firms have developed what is called a "moat around the business." They have the skills, information, contacts, and track record required to deliver. These qualities are hard to sustain and harder to replicate. It has become very hard to copycat them.

This kind of protected position is a valuable spot from which to negotiate economics. The major firms also benefit from investor consolidation, the demonstrated pattern of the largest investors, such as pension funds and sovereign wealth funds, concentrating their bets on an increasingly defined and often narrow set of blockbuster asset managers across the industry. These institutions buy bigger helpings of the private equity brands they like, in many of the investment strategies they sell. They are backing an established brand as much as they are backing an individual team or a specific fund. It is easier to repeat due diligence this way; if you back a known franchise, you do not need to start your due diligence from scratch each time and get to know the organization as well as the specific vehicle you are putting money into. It is the same in private equity as it would be for many other industries where the brand is key. If you are interested in a new smartphone, you will not feel silly walking into an Apple Store. If you want to shop online, Amazon is an excellent place to start browsing.

The same applies to the likes of KKR, Blackstone, Silver Lake, and Carlyle in private equity. These firms and others are the superstars who can raise capital more easily from a stable set of institutional investors than the rest of the industry. These "haves" do not have to scour the planet for checks in the same way less established firms might have to. They have a pipeline for fundraising and they are backed by investors who buy multiple products like leveraged buyout, credit, real estate, and infrastructure funds. They are always fundraising for one fund or another, and the investors often recycle profits from funds they previously invested in into new commitments.

The cycle works for both sides—the private equity firms have a plentiful well of capital to manage, and the investors are provided with a steady source of investment returns to service retirements. The private equity firms go all out with every tool at their disposal to achieve a superior return per unit of risk they take on for investors, and, given their liabilities, pension funds keep allocating to private equity and other private capital investment strategies. It is a symbiosis that keeps getting bigger.

In the previous two chapters, we have focused on the need to compete and win, and the benefits this competition can manifest for investors and private equity firms. In the next chapter, we turn to what can emerge from competitive hunger: the innovative spark to create and develop a new sector for investment. We have already mentioned insurance and credit investing as flourishing growth areas where private equity firms are steadily replacing traditional sources of capital. We now turn to a big sector where, until, say, twenty years ago, the largest alternative asset managers arguably had little interest. But today, this sector is of huge interest, partly owing to the enormous need for capital to replace aging public assets, particularly in developed economies. That sector is infrastructure. As is often the case with creative breakthroughs, the innovative spark came from somewhere unexpected.

# CHAPTER TEN

# Desperation, Not Hunger

"You're joking? How big is your fund?"

The Lehman Brothers banker snarls down at his office phone, scarcely concealing his contempt at having to take a call from a counterpart at a private equity fund he has never heard of, on the other side of the globe, in Sydney, Australia. From his corner office in Midtown Manhattan, the banker has seemingly reached close to the pinnacle of a city filled with finance professionals in search of big deals, fast money, and more power. His is a world of blacked-out limousines, expensive restaurants, and bespoke suits. It is 2003, and although the credit boom hints of a harsh reckoning in the years ahead, few stop to consider the possibility. Especially not this banker, who believes in the words and culture of his CEO with religious fervor. His wealth, $50 million on paper, is tied up in his employer's stock—and by the end of the decade it will be worthless.

He is an expert in mergers and acquisitions, and his cherished client is the best-known of the world's New York–based leveraged buyout firms. This established American private equity shop is the front-runner among a pack of rivals seeking to acquire an enormous portfolio of communications infrastructure assets to be carved out of European Broadcast Corporation, a venerable media giant that owns the largest and most influential TV and radio stations in Europe. On the block are broadcast towers and equipment required to transmit TV and radio signals over the air through the tower network as well as processing facilities to transform the media content produced in studios into transmissible broadcasts to send to viewers and listeners. Critically, the engineers and technical support staff who have run these activities are included in the transaction sale perimeter. They have decades of irreplaceable experience, and it will take many years to train new personnel to be able to take over their specialist roles.

For decades the prevailing thinking in the broadcast and media industries was that infrastructure and people were not separable from the creative content produced in the studios. The means of transmission had to sit alongside the folks who made the content, as part of the same company or group, like indivisible parts of an equation. Now, a rising wave of competition from cable companies and other forms of media with deep pockets has forced the conglomerate to rethink those assumptions. European Broadcast must consider ways to raise funds to compete effectively and maintain, if not grow, their audience appeal to the next generation of Internet-savvy customers. The solution being explored is to carve out the communications infrastructure and sell it as a standalone business. This will be a multi-billion-dollar deal.

The TV and radio stations of European Broadcast will become core customers for the new company to be carved out, with revenues and service levels governed by ten-year contracts with options to renew. As the stations are public service broadcasters, they are completely reliant on the communications infrastructure being sold to satisfy the national population coverage obligations in their broadcast licenses. Only this existing network of towers and facilities is broad and powerful enough to cover the entire population. Only this set of engineers and technical support staff can run the communications infrastructure. Installing fresh cable or fiber, for example, in every household would be too expensive. So, in effect, the TV and radio stations are captive clients. The private equity bidders see the attraction of stable revenues and cash flow, and together with drawing on lessons learned from investments in media and technology in other parts of their portfolios, they feel they understand the proposition. The Wall Street bank running the auction on behalf of European Broadcast, Goldman Sachs, has offered to underwrite junk bonds and loans for the winning bidder to finance the leveraged buyout. The deal will be the first of this kind, the carve-out of infrastructure and related assets from quasi-state entities, and, if successful, it will likely prompt a wave of similar transactions involving communications infrastructure assets in other markets.

It's the hottest deal of the new millennium. And yet rather than spend precious moments working with his Manhattan-based private equity client, the Lehman Brothers banker believes that he is wasting his time talking to this guy running a private equity fund out of Australia who also plans to bid for the same assets. Not just a bidder out of left field; someone from nowhere who seems not to realize his place in the financial pecking order. The Aussie had the guts to call the banker's American private equity client, and was politely directed to their advisors at Lehman Brothers. The banker is obliged to return the call out of professional courtesy—to his client—and because he knows that masters of private equity like to keep their options open. He pledges to give the guy five minutes.

On the phone, however, the Aussie is deadly serious. He explains to the Lehman Brothers banker that he is the head of a new investment vehicle set up by the largest Australian investment bank—one of the top ten banks in the Asia-Pacific region. It's a start-up private equity fund, but one with huge potential and a successful heritage. Sure, the Australian investment bank and its new fund are not well known in New York or London yet, but they are demonstrably successful, having completed similar infrastructure investments in Australia, and the call to the private equity firm was to discuss partnering on the communications infrastructure deal. The equity check is likely to be eight hundred million dollars, and, back in 2003, it was not uncommon for private equity firms to share this kind of sum and work together. As part of the value add, the Australian offers access to proprietary financing technology and operating insights that, apparently, have yet to reach New York or London. He claims to have an "edge" that will help the buyout firm *win*.

The Aussie proposes that both the equity check and the spoils from the investment be shared equally. The money, the fees, the returns, and the publicity for the deal. He suggests that the banker's American client hire the Australian bank as an equal co-advisor with Lehman Brothers, and that the two working groups should be joined at the hip, the two banks as advisors and the two funds as clients. Finally, he answers the Lehman Brothers banker's first question, the size of the fund; the vehicle only has two hundred million dollars at the moment, but it expects to raise the other two hundred million dollars required to fund half of the check through an equity capital markets issue to Australian pension funds, underwritten by the Australian bank, before the deal closes. The money is raised as it is needed, not in advance like a standard private equity fund, but there is nothing to be concerned about with this funding approach.

But the only thing the American banker hears is the current size of the fund, and after that, he switches off. *Two hundred million? All invested in one deal? And that's only half the money they need? What nonsense!* He does not think to ask more about the financing technology and operating insights that the Aussie is talking about. He is not thinking about what his private equity client would say to the proposal just outlined. In fact, he is not thinking at all. At this point, he is so certain that working with the Australian would be ridiculous, he feels that it is his responsibility to put him back in his place.

"Let me be clear. We would never partner with you. And we would never hire you. But thanks for the call, and good luck, pal."

This sketch is based on real events; what really happened was more brutal than the gentle fictionalization here. The folks from Australia were underestimated by many of the established financiers they met in New York and London. In one instance, I observed the partner of a well-known large private equity firm agree enthusiastically to discuss their ideas and approaches to working together, only to keep them waiting in a meeting room for over three hours. He then took voluminous notes during twenty minutes of discussion but later failed to return their calls over the next two months as the deal went live. Perhaps the Australians were a little naïve to think he would not act in this underhanded way.

What these financiers missed was that the Aussies were there out of desperation. That's the word their leadership used to describe the aching desire they felt to come up with something novel and effective. The killer app. Often the word *desperation* carries a negative connotation, but in this context, it means not just the hunger to succeed but also the primordial need to win—because failure would mean their start-up efforts to succeed against the world's major private equity firms might be shut down if they did not bear fruit. The Aussie was given a limited budget to run the start-up fund, some financial rope to play with, but his bosses' patience was limited. Unlike a major private equity fund, where partners have room to explore deals and incur some broken deal costs, the Aussie was working with a strict budget and living on borrowed time. He had no brand name to hide behind and he could not hand out impressive business cards. He rode the subway and flew coach. He didn't have the luxury of waiting three years to do one good deal. He only had a smart idea.

What was this idea? Put simply, the Australians, in their home market, had proven experience in investing in and financing this type of "hard asset" or "infrastructure asset." They had developed a way to present assets such as TV and mobile network towers, airports and ports, toll roads and turnpikes to potential lenders as safer than operating businesses that private equity firms typically acquire, chemicals companies and healthcare businesses and the like. They convinced lenders that the investment strategy for these assets was to hold them for the long term, at least ten years, and to extract dividends from the ample cash flow they would generate over this horizon, rather than sell them for a quick profit.

One day, the "infrastructure" assets might be sold at the right price, but there was no pressure to exit. In fact, the Australian funds' own investors, such as local pension funds, were attracted to the idea of steady dividends over a long horizon.

Having won this argument, they were able to apply the debt financing technology used in project finance—such as building toll roads—to leveraged buyouts of this new breed of so-called infrastructure assets. This debt financing technology involved the use of higher levels of cheaper debt than would normally be permitted in a leveraged buyout, reflecting the perception that infrastructure assets—if properly run—were far safer than lending to or underwriting the acquisition financing of "ordinary" leveraged buyouts. It was clever spin, but it was based on substance. And of all the suitors chasing the European Broadcast deal, the Aussies' angle was the dark horse of the auction, because most of the other bidders dismissed their approach as naïve, plain wrong, or a mix of both.

The Australians had the vision to foresee that the world's largest investors in private equity funds—massive pension funds and sovereign wealth funds with hundreds of billions of dollars that needed a home to generate investment returns—would soon flock to the "infrastructure" sector. Why? Because these kinds of assets often have attributes that are attractive to investors looking for safe but high-earning homes for their cash. They often involve hard physical assets that are difficult to build and replace, and often require licenses or leases or concessions to operate. They often feature revenues underpinned by long-term contracts, barriers to entry for competitors, big profit margins, capital expenditures that can be planned years in advance, and plentiful cash flow to pay regular dividends and service high levels of cheap debt.

Service-level agreements between the infrastructure asset operators like an airport and clients, such as airlines, tend to be strict and come with heavy penalties for breaches. All parties involved have a lot to lose if something goes wrong, not to mention bad headlines and regulatory scrutiny. In many cases, the assets are considered to be essential utilities, so they are very unlikely to go out of business. A deal involving infrastructure assets can be financed with lower-interest and longer-term debt much more cheaply than a leveraged buyout and use more leverage than a buyout. That meant more cheap debt used, less equity on the hook from investors, and more upside if it worked out.

The financing "technology" imagined by the Australians included concepts not commonly used in buyouts, such as purchasing credit insurance to make the debt appear safer—thereby lowering the interest payments due—and relying on the large project finance arms of Main Street banks, who were grateful just to be part of the big deals that Wall Street banks typically dominated. Main Street bankers received millions of dollars in fees, and found themselves working on deal after deal in infrastructure. An area previously considered deeply unattractive, even boring, was booming.

That's what had gotten the Australians interested in European Broadcast. The trick was to identify the towers and associated assets from this target as a group of assets that could pass as infrastructure. Their vision was to package them, finance them, and ultimately run them as a long-term, stable business paying out healthy dividends because they had the attributes to support this vision. The public service broadcasters that constituted the client base were dependent on the tower infrastructure to provide TV and radio signals to the population, to provide continuity of universal service, as required in the licenses that permitted them to function. There was no question of non-payment, given that the broadcasters were supported by state bodies in Western democracies; they were AAA-rated clients. Safe as houses.

The due diligence executed by the Australian team was more comprehensive than anything that Goldman Sachs, the Wall Street bank running the sale, had ever seen. They were thorough to the point of being paranoid that they would miss something important—and relentless. The team built a comprehensive picture of the target's revenues and cash flow from the ground up, contract by contract. They did not rely on lawyers or consultants to summarize the contractual terms; they read them individually themselves to make sure. Nobody tried to hover at thirty thousand feet, and nobody thought they were so senior they could skip the all-night calls needed to prosecute a transaction across two hemispheres. From this bottom-up analysis of the revenue order book to the cost structure, every layer of earnings was scrutinized. How predictable is the cash flow? What is the credit rating of the client? Is it essential for the customer to renew? Can pricing be increased during the agreement? When is it renewed and on what terms? Where can we improve costs? Are there other tower assets we can buy as bolt-on acquisitions after this deal closes? Debates raged over assigning a different cost of capital to contracted versus optional revenue, over secure versus potential cash flow. And it was all done with dry wit.

The Australians had a point to prove. Having faced hubris and ego from the established operators on Wall Street, the newcomers pushed each other to work harder, think smarter, and act sharper. They were proud that they did not have an established brand to rely on when they scoured the globe for investments. You got a desk, a laptop, and a phone. There were no offices. Even the CEO of the Australian bank sat among the troops (although he allowed himself to permanently reserve a small meeting room for confidential calls). Senior dealmakers in London and New York were often disturbed at night with aggressive if good-natured exhortations from the center of Sydney.

"Wake up, lazy! Sleep *after* winning!"

This is what desperation looked like—what it took to succeed in rebranding buyouts as "infrastructure" investments. If the deal team could pull this off, they would then be able to persuade lenders that the risk of default for such investments was minimal—more like the risk associated with a toll road or a bridge than an ordinary leveraged buyout by a private equity firm. The investment could then be financed more like a project to construct or maintain a critical piece of national infrastructure than financed like a leveraged buyout. To put this into numerical perspective: For this kind of deal in 2003, junk bonds required roughly eight percent interest, and sixty percent of the purchase price could be debt-financed. But if the investment were recast as "infrastructure," the interest rate could be as low as three percent, and leverage could make up eighty percent of the deal price. A "safer" deal, with more debt and less equity needed.

Under this scenario, with less of the cash flow generated by the target going to pay interest on the acquisition debt, more of it could be used to pay frequent distributions to investors, known as a running cash yield. And with less equity in the deal in the first place and more debt, this secure river of cash every month or quarter would boost the return on that lower amount of equity put in.

What this meant was that the Australians, locked in the race to win an auction against traditional private equity bidders, could afford to give up some of that boosted return by paying a higher purchase price. It meant they could win. And if they really believed the asset carried lower risk than a leveraged buyout, they would target a lower return in the first place; say, an annual return of fifteen percent, rather than the twenty percent or more that private equity typically aims for. Add all this up—the impact of a running cash yield, less equity, and lower expected returns associated with lower perceived risk, and a competitor taking the infrastructure approach could blow away a traditional private equity firm in an auction while still making money handsomely and providing an attractive return to investors.

That is precisely what happened with European Broadcast. The leveraged buyout shops brought knives to a gunfight, with predictable results. The creative folks from Australia not only won the deal; they began winning deal after deal, an advantage that endured for years. It took time for traditional private equity firms to believe that the advantage was real, not some transient black box, and to learn how to copy and enhance it. There were many skeptics at private equity firms who thought the whole thing would fall apart like a house of cards. Surely, they were lucky, not better.

For the Australians, the advantages of the "infrastructure approach" stretched beyond acquisition financing to understanding the operations of the European Broadcast tower assets as well. Prior experience with infrastructure assets in Australia, from toll roads to communications towers, meant that when it came to negotiating the key revenue contracts the team had a further edge. They already spoke the language of this new sector, including how to index revenues to inflation, lower costs through outsourcing, and make sure capital expenditures were financed efficiently and earned an adequate return. They already had a network of executives and experts able to help with diligence and run targets post-acquisition. They already knew how to structure and negotiate separation and transition agreements in deals where infrastructure assets were being carved out of groups, as was the case with European Broadcast.

Furthermore, as the horizon of the business plan was longer-term than the standard five years of a leveraged buyout, the Australians presented themselves as different from private equity firms when pitching to buy assets from governments, as the sellers of national infrastructure through privatizations or other sale processes. They looked good in front of regulators. Here was a bidder who not only paid top dollar but also had operating know-how and did not need to sell out soon.

Today, infrastructure is a core part of the private capital industry, and each of the major firms offers fund vehicles that invest in different parts of the sector including transportation, energy and utilities, water and waste, communications and digital infrastructure, power generation, and renewables.

It is true that investment returns have often come down for infrastructure assets in the past two decades since the events that inspired our sketch, partly because so many other actors have gotten in on the act. Essential services and utility assets are not always expected to generate the same annual investment returns that private equity deals can typically generate, unless there are particular complexities or sets of risks associated with them— such as they went wrong and are acquired out of bankruptcy, or the target is a mix of an infrastructure asset with other, "riskier" assets that make the investment less stable and predictable than an infrastructure investment.

What is also true in the past twenty years is that investment professionals focusing on infrastructure assets have at times learned painful lessons, committing to deals that ended up not being infrastructure after all. In many cases these investments were the victims of too much spin. Many of these deals were in reality ordinary leveraged buyouts with the infrastructure label stretched to the breaking point. Businesses ranging from yellow pages to vacation ferries to parking lots to fixed-line telephone companies were at one time touted as essential assets and services by overzealous would-be dealmakers. Many had to be restructured after facing difficulties, such as the impact of technology and unforeseen changes in the competitive environment or customer demand. Conversely, assets that were almost snapped up but evaded the grasp of infrastructure bidders, such as stock exchanges, could have worked out well if the infrastructure folks had managed to get ahold of them.

The sector has now matured as it has grown, having learned through these mistakes, and it is served by many investment firms—both the major private equity firms and those specializing in infrastructure alone. We are at the point where category integrity is less likely to be an issue going forward than it was during the sector's earlier phase of growth. And as geopolitics has grown to be more complex, with polarized politics and a reshaping of alliances, the importance of national infrastructure has only made the space more appealing for investors to have exposure to, from pipelines to grids for energy and power, from water supply to airports, and from data centers to other forms of technology infrastructure. Infrastructure is here to stay.

Like the importance of raw intelligence and forward thinking on display with insurance investments, we can now add a dose of *desperation* to the traits that pave the way to long-term success for the masters of private equity. Desperation can lead to being genuinely innovative in a way that competitors would struggle to grasp. For the Australians, it was a way to put their franchise on the map. To beat the usual suspects on Wall Street and gain acceptance to the club. For them, ordinary hunger to succeed was *not enough*.

How lucrative was it to be desperate? The infrastructure pioneers were not just innovators when it came to a new sector. They were equally creative when it came to delivering on economics for themselves as well as for their investors. The investment bank behind the investment vehicle was publicly listed, not unlike the major private equity firms of today. The infrastructure funds charged their investors a variation of Two and Twenty, much like the major private equity funds of today. And there were deal fees for making the investments, fees for financing or refinancing assets, monitoring fees for participating in board meetings and working on the business plans of investee companies, and deal fees for exiting the investments. Often, the infrastructure investments were sold to a similar set of local pension fund investors who had backed the investment vehicle itself at the start.

The establishment of infrastructure as an asset class for private capital has had another benefit for private equity—the development of a new analytical lens for investment professionals to use when looking at a potential target, even if the opportunity is *outside* the infrastructure sector. When looking at private equity deals or at distressed debt, the infrastructure know-how acquired by firms empowers deal teams to ask about the hard assets that are in—or could be added to—the target perimeter, to think differently about the barriers to market entry and customer switching, to consider the reliance of clients, and to scrutinize the security and stability of revenues and cash flow, including the structure of client contracts and renewal options. The defensive attributes of an investment, or its weaknesses, can be looked at better because of the addition of this savoir faire. Much the same way that the lens added by a real estate fund would help ask questions about property or that a firm with credit expertise can look at a buyout target and critique the capital structure.

And with the cost of capital, or expected returns, lower in the infrastructure sector versus private equity, generally, private equity folks now have an additional tool to consider how to shape and influence the strategic plan underpinning a business when they consider making an investment. Do we need to buy the supporting infrastructure for this company, or can we lease it? Can we get the hard assets for a bargain, as they are underloved? Might we be able to carve up this part of a target and dispose of it to an infrastructure bidder who would pay a higher price for it as they only need a lower return for it? Can we buy a business, sell off the non-infrastructure bits, and position the bulk of what is left as infrastructure for a strong exit?

The deal surgeons now have another scalpel in their arsenal to dissect a situation. This franchise effect across a private equity firm compounds further when two products combine—for example, infrastructure and credit. Firms now think of infrastructure investing not just as a distinct sector for buyouts and carve-outs but also as a hunting ground for debt opportunities. The credit funds look at investing in the debt of infrastructure deals, whether performing or distressed, and of course this requires infrastructure expertise. Infrastructure has served as a source of fuel for the growth of the credit funds managed by private equity firms.

Beyond financial rewards and franchise benefits, another consequence of innovation in the private equity industry concerns information. Each time a new sector or product is created, the data collected on that part of the economy augments the massive reservoirs of numbers and facts held by the private equity firms and their portfolio companies. This includes information on target companies, their sectors, their competitors, their clients, their suppliers, and often their key people. Private equity firms also have data on sectors and targets regarding financial performance, operating metrics, regulatory problems, and due diligence issues. The information is collected through the investment strategies—private equity, credit, infrastructure, real estate, and so on. Data you might not think a private equity firm has—from businesses as diverse as the dating app you may use to the dentist you might visit.

This well of knowledge within a private equity firm—continuously updated and managed to prevent conflicts of interest—is distilled for use by a firm's investment professionals. Deal teams can draw on lessons learned from the pursuit of targets in related sectors of the economy. For example, a chemicals company can have insight on the food packaging business it sells to. A hospital chain can shed light on the medical supplies provider it relies on. A food retail group has data on the weekly shopping of its customers and the agricultural sectors that supply it with fresh produce. Every deal, each year, a private equity firm's expertise grows as its data harvesting deepens.

Ultimately, this process of distilling knowledge is about gaining an edge. It can teach the aspiring master of private equity when to say no when it is vital to let a poor investment idea die, and when to push for yes when there is real conviction backed up by a persuasive fact pattern. In the next chapter, we will go deeper into this information edge, revealing how data collection and use is increasingly vital to delivering the investment returns that pension funds and other investors rely on. We will see that private equity is, in a sense, always watching.

# CHAPTER ELEVEN

# The Library

No conflict, no interest.

Imagine you control a conglomerate with business holdings across the world. This group is a major private equity firm plus the companies that its managed funds control or have significant influence in, across multiple investment strategies for private capital. Private equity, credit, real estate, infrastructure, and so on. It's a gigantic business. You are or have invested in nearly every sector of the economy: aerospace and defense, consumer and retail, media and telecom, real estate and infrastructure, energy and utilities, banks and insurance, business and consumer services, healthcare and pharmaceuticals, industrials and manufacturing, transportation and travel, and technology. Your empire includes over three hundred individual investments in over two hundred companies, together employing hundreds of thousands of workers. And you are an *active* manager of these businesses, with your top deal guys governing each one from a position of material influence, such as the board of directors.

Your scale and network are so vast and powerful that in addition to your sector deal teams, you maintain and have access to a team of corporate executives to serve as operational managers for investments. These experts help each portfolio company get leaner, make better decisions faster, and execute transformation initiatives. From strategy and business plans to senior executive and non-executive hiring to investing in technology and systems as a competitive differentiator and an enabler of problem-solving, your teams are on standby, ready to jump in and tackle thorny issues. Your job is not at thirty thousand feet, however. You must also be prepared to help with the micro topics that reduce risk and raise return, including optimization of tax structuring, data collection and storage, accounting and audit functions, procurement and cost savings, healthcare plans for employees, cybersecurity and IT systems, energy efficiency and emissions reduction, public relations and government liaison, and so on.

You are everywhere, but you cannot get lost in the weeds. Partnering with executive management at each holding, you focus on the major levers that drive making money, on the key factors in a target's business plan that can create value for your investors and for yourself. You don't confuse your own role, as an investor and the ultimate decision-maker in the enterprises your funds have invested in, with the role of the management teams at each of these holdings. You can operate from the board or dig in deeper, as is usually required, to help make your investments as successful as they can be.

How can you achieve all of this? A key part of your success is that you are amassing a vast pool of data. On trends in revenue and cost in your investments and those you passed up. On patterns of customer and supplier and competitor behavior. On profitable capital expenditure projects and smart acquisitions with synergies. What improves operations and what does not. Lists and profiles of top talent in management.

You collect this information in different ways, giving you different lenses on the incoming data. Sometimes you own a supplier to another industry and learn about how your customers behave. Other times you buy one of the very same customers and recall how to handle suppliers—because you used to own one. Frequently, you are in different parts of the value chain *at the same time.* You are growing at such a pace that you could end up with an investment in several players in the same industry, some of whom might compete with one another directly. In this case, perhaps your investments are not all of the same form: You could own one player outright through a leveraged buyout in one fund, but in one of its rivals, in another one of your funds, you could own part of the debt that sits in its capital structure. A little here, a lot there.

The data from each investment is probably not public, so you have to manage the information carefully to avoid conflicts of interest across your empire, using strict information barriers between funds that you police very well. At some level in your organization, some of the most senior folks may sit above these information barriers, and they will still be able to navigate this data gold mine, because it's part of their leadership function. It is part of their role to consider when to create and keep information silos and when *not* to. They are quite used to this function and possible tension. They do it well, time and again, until these nuances become second nature.

Over the years, hundreds of billions of dollars pour into your group from investors, and you research scores of potential deals each year. You keep learning. Synapses fire, and you become more and more adept at connecting the dots between the data you gather. Of course, you maintain the integrity of where the information came from and keep the promises made in non-disclosure agreements. You delete the files and financial models as requested by counterparties when an investment you are analyzing falls through. You are cautious about how to handle incoming data from rivals, and you employ powerful internal checks to handle compliance and regulatory matters. But although you are able to shred physical files, and even if you handle the data appropriately, it is hard to *unlearn* what you have learned. You cannot wipe clean the minds of your investment professionals, seasoned as they are in analyzing data, as if they are hard drives. You cannot push the learning process backward. Just by examining deals, as well as doing them, you gain valuable investing experience—including sector expertise and contacts with management teams. And your picture about the macro-economy sharpens markedly, too. You develop deep knowledge about the state of the economy by analyzing its component parts. You have an edge.

Once you have that edge, you do not stop. You do not stand still; you invest in data science and machine learning to harness more of the power of the information you gather. And when you combine that power with your track record for investing and the enormous reserves of cash you have on tap to do deals, you start to outpace your rivals more and more. It is a virtuous circle, with the odd mishap along the way, a deal here or there that fails and can't be salvaged.

The picture I've painted above is not too far off from where the major private equity firms are now. In each firm, investment professionals have access to detailed information on deals that are live, companies that have already been sold, businesses that were examined but not invested in, and the perspectives of executives involved in every situation. Relative to the quantum of funds under management, the size of the group with access to this material is small. And they're learning more with every project.

In truth, what we are talking about is not just data but intelligence. From each holding, the management teams and the private equity professionals involved collect key performance indicators and information that act like a live webcam on the investment and the ecosystem around the deal—from suppliers to customers to competitors to regulators. This information populates a dashboard about that investment. Adding these dashboards up, the private equity firm can tell which way the wind is blowing, or even which way it might blow, regarding not only the companies invested in but also their rivals and the sectors they operate in. It's like having giant monitors in front of you to keep an eye on large parts of the economy, with images updated in real time.

How is consumer sentiment? What is the climate for investing in a specific sector or niche? Which risk factors do management teams fear the most? Executives at portfolio companies, past and present, are polled on macro questions, and their replies help to reveal the direction of travel in industries across the economy. This type of data intelligence, what I call "the library" of a private equity firm, is an incredibly potent weapon, and it has started to incorporate elements of automation. Systems can churn out quarterly flash numbers for supply and demand or regular updates of how a specific portfolio business is progressing and the key trends in its sector. And the larger the funds and the bigger the portfolios, the greater the data and the better the insight. The bigger the edge for investing better.

Given that private equity involves making a careful, balanced wager on a deal idea, the analytical rigor that underpins the investment work is vital. And knowing what to ask is just as important as what you already know. Financial models that drive the analysis of risk versus return are grounded in the information that comes through due diligence work by the deal team and third-party advisors, including lawyers and accountants. There are usually multiple bidders for each target, whether they are organized through a formal auction or quiet conversations, and in most cases, a prime differentiating factor of the work conducted by each bidder can be the quality of intelligence they have on the target's sector, including the target and its competitors. The closer the bidder is to the numbers that map what is happening most accurately in a deal, the higher the chances of success. You might be forgiven for thinking that to have the best inside view of a target's prospects, you almost have to be *too close* to the situation. Close enough that your knowledge makes you, in a sense, an insider to the target even before you sign the check. You have an interest, and if you are not careful, you might (almost) have a conflict. This has to be managed.

Put differently, what will separate bidders for a target is partly their intelligence around the investment, because it will drive a business plan they have conviction in and believe is likely to work when executed by the management team that they are backing to run the target. And so the firm with the best-stocked "library" may well be the one with the best chance to win. The firm that has been watching and gathering data, possibly for years through its broader portfolio and deal activities. The firm with the cameras always set to "record." And as with nearly everything in private equity, this intelligence process starts with and revolves around the *people* who animate the system. It's the people who invest in those cameras, who calibrate the data, and who assess the intelligence from them that help investments succeed.

"It's great to see old friends—and some new friends too."

The Founder makes some perfunctory opening remarks at the

Firm's annual meeting of its investors in Manhattan. It is 2021. The grand conference rooms at the five-star Four Seasons Hotel on Fifth Avenue are packed, and the hotel is sold out for the two-night, three-day private event. In attendance are the Firm's partners and investment professionals as well as the CEOs and chairs of the portfolio companies that the funds are invested in, primarily through the private equity group but also across the credit, infrastructure, and real estate teams. Most of the guests have flown in especially for this event, from all over the globe. For the first time in the Firm's forty-year history, the industry executives outnumber the deal guys by *five to one*. This ratio is a reflection of the Firm's reach and relentless growth. Bigger funds, more deals, more portfolio businesses, more experts, and more intelligence.

Over the next fifty hours of meetings and working meals prepared by the hotel's chefs, the Firm will review the macro climate for investing, assess where it has an advantage over rivals, and revisit the performance of the funds—including the largest portfolio companies they are invested in. Group heads will present the numbers and take questions as the marketing teams film appealing snippets for the website and social media. The odd senior banker is present, invited as a reward for good investment-banking coverage of the deal folks, including making sure leverage is available when needed, especially when markets are choppy. There is a handful of friendly journalists. But for the most part this is an exclusive forum. Security is heavy; the hotel is swarming with humorless guards in dark suits and earpieces. The sidewalks outside the hotel are lined with blacked-out SUVs.

The conference costs millions of dollars to organize and execute. The Firm's investment professionals in overseas offices are motivated by the opportunity to be in New York for one-to-one meetings with the Firm's leaders. But their costs pale in comparison to what it costs to gather so many senior business executives together in one go. First-class tickets on commercial airlines or private jets and five-star hotels are the norm. The funds pay for some of these costs, which means that ultimately, some of it gets charged back to investors, and the Firm pays for the rest. However, regardless of cost, the value to be gained from brainstorming sessions in breakout rooms, and cultivating contacts across the investment portfolio, will be essential for originating new deals and running live ones.

Of course, not every executive knows the others beforehand. Some of the investments are new, whereas others are nearing exit after an extended period of ownership. The investors love to mingle with the top folks in each sector of the economy, hear what is really happening behind the key numbers, and consider the implications for their commitments to the Firm's funds— and to funds managed by other private equity firms. For a few days, they get closer to the dealmaking action than they are likely to be for the rest of the year.

And so the annual meeting serves as a massive networking event as well as a marketing showpiece for raising new funds. The conference exudes a special chemistry, fueled by the mix of superstar presence from the Founder, representatives from the largest pension funds in the world and other major investors, and some of the top global business executives. All of these constituents are affiliated with the Firm, all are insiders in a way, and all are reliant on or have contributed to the investment performance of the Firm's funds. What is striking about the gathering is not only the motivations of the individuals present but the power of the information they exchange and the web of data they control—whether it is to be harnessed during the gathering or subsequently. For each sector, each company, each rival, and each business counterparty, the Firm can tap into intelligence regarding deals—live or proposed—that might come up within the matrix of its contacts.

The Founder's comments are peppered with a curated set of data that supports his personal take on the flash reports of information from the Treasury regarding inflation, unemployment, and economic growth. He frames the figures against a backdrop of geopolitical issues and opines on a band of outcomes for the economy. This is no place for sitting on the fence; his views are clear, thoughtful, and nuanced. And as he concludes and the presentations roll on, what the Firm is really doing is setting the scene for the deal meetings that will follow, in breakout talks at the hotel or remotely in the weeks ahead, on ways to make money for investors and for itself.

Of special interest this year is a batch of sessions put together by one of the deal teams. The deal team is working on a project that would involve a two-billion-dollar carve-out of a scientific publishing business from the largest global publisher of educational textbooks for college students and research papers. The target publishes core science curriculum textbooks, study workbooks, and practice exam questions as well as academic journals in several fields, from nuclear physics to climate change to the study of pandemics. The target markets are North America and Europe. At present, the business is wholly owned by a North American conglomerate, but the parent company needs money to fund its expansion in Asia, where growth is booming. Although the science publishing division is highly cash-generative, it is low-growth and is viewed as having limited opportunity. The conglomerate's stock is publicly listed, and

Wall Street bankers have long argued that the science publishing division, however lucrative, is holding back if not depressing the conglomerate's valuation metrics. If the science publishing division could be sold, the conglomerate could be repositioned as a growth play on the higher education industry in emerging markets and get quickly re-rated to a much higher valuation.

The problem is disclosure. Reporting guidelines do not require the group to reveal the science publishing division's profitability or cost structure. Wall Street bankers struggle to estimate accurately the profit margins on each revenue unit within the science publishing division. Perhaps to deflect criticism of profiteering from academics and universities, it is hard to pinpoint a reliable estimate for the cash flow numbers. Without this raw data, putting a reliable value on the science publishing division, in practical terms, will be impossible. But fortunately, the private equity folks at the Firm have assembled a team of senior executives from past and current investments that might be able to unlock the situation and set a deal in motion.

Three years ago, the Firm's private equity fund invested in a group of for-profit law and finance colleges that successfully made the transition to online schooling, massively reducing paper and print costs and increasing flexibility and choice for students working to gain professional qualifications. The company is now likely to be sold within the next two years at a profit of more than double the purchase price. Six years earlier, the Firm's credit fund had scored another winner, exiting a home-run debt investment in a specialist publisher of textbooks and academic research for medical practitioners that had temporarily stumbled due to an accounting scandal. And, as a personal investment outside of the Firm, the Founder owns a must-read business and economics magazine that is respected all over the world. Online learning, medical publishing, and a specialty magazine—seven executives from all of these targets have gathered in a private breakout room at the Firm's annual meeting, forming a powerful quorum to assist the Firm with its evaluation of the science publishing opportunity.

Together with the Firm's deal team, the executives gathered form the Firm's working group for the deal. The deal team presents the potential investment, reviewing the seller's situation and quickly progressing to the numbers and the questions and issues that still need to be resolved. They have revenues for each unit of the science publishing division and a total operating profit line that evidences the target's contribution to the conglomerate's aggregated cash flow. But the deal team needs to estimate the division's income and cash flow statements, plus balance sheet items and working capital detail, all on a standalone basis, as if the target existed outside its parent group, in order to estimate the target's ability to generate cash and pay for the high-yield acquisition debt they intend to raise in a leveraged buyout. The deal team needs to estimate how far it could push its pricing strategy to drive profit margins and what costs can be trimmed.

How do they do it? Collectively, the seven management executives in the room have over two hundred years of publishing experience. They and the Firm have the data from the investments they have been or are involved with. They turn that data into intelligence for the Firm. They are not there to consult as salaried experts—as a consulting firm might employ them to do. They are there as part of the stars in the Firm's orbit, to prosecute its agenda, as if they are personally involved in managing the target. They take ownership and relish the chance to demonstrate the value they can add *with an investor's mindset.* They do not sit on the fence, nor do they make arguments for and against the transaction so deliberately balanced that the advice ends up lacking direction. They attack the task. And so, using initial impressions from their experience and rounds of calls they have made to contacts across the science publishing sector, they convey preliminary views to create a box around what is known and to identify the unknowns that remain and need to be addressed. They focus on what could go wrong, what is likely to boost profit margins, how best to profit from digital transition, and what has worked best during the pandemic. They help set up the work plan to steer the next stage of their input as well as frame the work for granular due diligence reports to be commissioned from accountants, tax advisors, and consultants. The executives are part of a Rolodex you can't buy or hire.

By serving as an extension of the deal team, the senior executives act as a human extension of the Firm's library, one that other bidders will not be able to replicate, certainly at this early stage of the project. They are able to use their contacts, scour the available data from past and live deals, and help the Firm come up with a realistic band of outcomes for what the financials of the target could be, including projections for profits and cash flow a few years out. What this means is that they are able to help the Firm create a realistic, if only approximate, financial picture of the science publishing division as it would be acquired by the private equity fund—even before they have received any information from the seller. It enables the deal team to bid proactively, to put the asset in play. Inevitably, there will be competition for a target of this size, but with this approach, the Firm will be able to take a commanding, though not unbeatable, lead in any sale process that might follow. The Firm can be *first,* and in this position, it can be the first to decide if the target is worth the reserve price that the seller is demanding. It will have time to rework the key pieces of information that the final bid price will be based on—the business plan, the acquisition debt financing, the target's management team, and the need for fresh talent at the management and board level. It can also signal to the market that something serious is amiss if it decides to withdraw.

And, of course, the lineup of experts adds credibility. Selling out to private equity can be a political nightmare in socially sensitive sectors, such as education. Financiers are not typically known for their scientific acumen. An exit to a private equity firm, even a large and powerful one, is possibly a less controversial transaction when the deal folks are genuinely working with some of the brightest and most decorated leaders in the target's industry. Surely, these industry executives will have done their homework about the firm they are affiliated with and are consenting to be seen with. Surely, there will be no cashing out through leveraging up with debt. Surely, it's legitimate and clear. A seller considering a complicated, lengthy carve-out to private equity would take comfort from the bench that surrounds and guides the buyer.

The halo effect extends beyond the seller, to trade unions, counterparties such as colleges and government administrators, and ultimately, students. If textbook and research prices rise following a deal with private equity, the ecosystem around a socially sensitive sector will rightly ask questions about what is driving the price increases: profit hunting or product investment? A rise in wages for textbook authors or a big dividend to multimillionaires and billionaires in private equity—and to the pension funds that rely on their returns? Or is it a bit of everything? A private equity firm is better prepared and better positioned with respected folks from the industry lending their time, their expertise, and their names.

Beyond contacts, the working group has a data library to

support the views they hold. Some of the executives have been involved in multiple buyouts or carve-outs, and they know well both the rules of thumb and specific pieces of key information that can make or break a new investment. All of those assembled have been through scores of virtual and physical data rooms in their careers, across multiple deals in education or publishing. What they are doing now is framing the investment for the Firm in terms of the likely financial picture that will emerge during due diligence.

Four weeks pass after the conference, and the intelligence edge that the quorum provides results in a period of exclusivity for the Firm to sign a transaction. The seller is impressed with the depth and strength of the Firm's bench, the all-star cast, and the accuracy and speed with which the deal team has looked at the target. It is as if they have been a fly on the wall for years; the preliminary indication of interest submitted by the deal partner showed that the basic economics of the science publishing division were boxed correctly into a realistic zone, and the proposed price recognized the room to create value under new ownership. There are other bidders, of course, but none come as close to hitting the sweet spot, the nexus of being credible as the new custodian of an important asset in a socially sensitive sector *and* delivering on an attractive valuation. The Firm is the standout winner.

At present, the science publishing division is not a stand-alone entity, and so the parties agree to a long period between the signing and the closing of the deal in order to allow due time for a safe and comprehensive separation of functions and transition to an independent, healthy existence. After the deal is announced and the initial burst of media attention fades, it seems as if the transaction has entered a somewhat boring phase for both sides. But it is during this downtime that the library of people and numbers will work the hardest for the Firm. It is now that the library will help make the most money for the Firm and its investors, by providing the deal team with a further edge.

What the seller is missing is that the period between signing a deal and closing it for a carve-out is the ideal time for private equity to drive a harder bargain. After signing, the senior executives from the seller withdraw to some extent, leaving their transaction lieutenants to attend to the less glamorous task of defining the precise transaction perimeter for separating target assets from the parent and organizing transitional periods and costs for services the science publishing division currently relies on. Think IT systems, accounting and taxes, client data, supplier information, capital expenditures, regulatory liaison—the web of functions that is critical for a standalone company to operate. In contrast, that is where the Firm's working group leans in. Every minute aspect of the carve-out is analyzed, including how much working capital and cash are assigned to the target at closing. Every material detail of the transition arrangements and separation contracts is negotiated. The quorum knows that this is where the real price of the transaction will be revealed, where the Firm will be able to drive a wedge between the more seller-friendly headline price and the price actually paid. For this investment, the delta ends up as a ten percent discount, taking down the valuation from what was reasonable to a lower level that the Firm regards as a smart bargain.

Under the radar, the library has acted as a second skin for private equity. It has added intelligence to outdo competing bidders and bench strength to outdo the seller. The library, the deal team, and the executives have likely created a home run for the private equity fund by extracting value from the science publishing division, raising prices where they can, boosting profit margins, expanding product lines, reducing costs, and making for a lucrative investment. The library is an essential part of the mix.

This deal is not an isolated example—as a private equity firm grows, its library expands and deepens, with incoming data from buyouts, carve-outs, and debt investments across nearly all sectors of the economy. What all this means is that increasingly, as private equity gets bigger, the intelligence that its professionals gather plays a bigger role in tilting the odds in their favor.

In this chapter, we're beginning to see how the model of private equity works on the macro level. It creates a virtuous cycle for the firms that perform: intelligence, then deals, then bigger funds, then more investments, and back to intelligence. The library is a crucial component to create this cycle. Of course, there are plenty of other industries where experts are called in to help with specific projects, but the difference in private equity comes in both the scale and the nature of the activities. For a private equity fund's investors, this is a good thing—the professionals they rely on to make investment returns can be exceptionally well informed and are often able to analyze and conclude a deal worth billions of dollars within a few months. And think of it this way: The inevitability of *having* to exit an investment, one way or another, in order to make money puts more pressure on the quality and comprehensiveness of the information needed at the time the investment is made. With each investment, private equity builds on what was learned in prior deals—they are in this for the long haul, like their investors. The library gets better every day.

In the next chapter, we return to the investment committee of a private equity fund. We'll witness a discussion on a complex deal where a private equity firm creates favorable conditions for success by stacking the odds in their own favor—of course, in part by using its library. We'll see the masters of private equity at the top of their game, engaged in an investment process that is designed to systematically drive up their chances of winning, step by step.

# CHAPTER TWELVE

# Stack the Deck

"I have no interest in a fair fight."

The Founder's words set the tone at the start of the weekly investment committee meeting. He is speaking in blunt, plain terms, and yet to the casual observer his words might seem coded. He is not talking about cheating. He is referring to the investment process the Firm excels at, the way the Firm analyzes prospective investments. He means that the odds of winning must be high, certainly in the Firm's favor, for a deal to be approved in this forum. By the point at which it reaches the committee, the investment idea must be sufficiently developed that, if approved to proceed, it is much more likely to happen than not. The deal team will have looked carefully at every material risk and opportunity, examining them if not resolving them, dispassionately and without fear. There cannot be any holes. And even if the initial structure of the project is lacking something, the deal team must have made the effort to remold the transaction to improve it. What he expects is that the deck of cards should have been worked by now, stacked, for the idea to be interesting. He expects the library to have been used fully. The Founder has no patience for a broad auction where winning means a spin of the roulette wheel.

If the professionals have done their jobs, the number of deals brought to the investment committee that fail to materialize will be limited, because the proposals are so well prepared. Failed bids and broken deal costs must be minimized. The Firm focus on investments that make money.

The Founder is right to have these demands, of course. The teams are paid to examine deals and make the solid ones happen—and then execute them well. The Firm has forty years of experience; it has made one hundred investments and has performed well ninety times—having exited already or being positioned in line for a profitable exit in a few years, where the return adequately compensates for the risks being taken. The remaining ten are either mistakes, returning nothing to investors, or deals where the future looks challenging but it's too early to tell the likely outcome.

A win rate of at least ninety percent is roughly the sweet spot—and in some vintages, the Firm has done even better. Ninety percent feels commensurate with Two and Twenty, with the high fees the masters of private equity command. If the best odds of success you can muster are fifty/fifty, you are not part of the elite in the industry. If your proposed transaction does not complete, it should be because the seller has pulled out—maybe irrationally—which suggests the possibility that they might come back later, or because another bidder has paid a price for the asset that your analysis did not support. These exceptions aside, the compelling attributes of your proposal—valuation, speed, experience, and network—should be enough to win.

The Firm's investment process that leads to these results can appear to be brutal. The investment professionals map each deal in terms of the likely band of outcomes for risk and return. The key pillars of every project are distilled into what you need to believe to maximize the returns per unit of risk and what you must do to turn the theory into reality, the potential into the kinetic. This means asking the tough questions, tearing a project apart. It means acting as forensic investigators to deconstruct an idea into a series of critical assumptions that need data to back them up and an execution plan to implement action items. The deal team will expose weaknesses in the investment thesis, determining what can be supported through diligence and what needs to be addressed through the terms of the transaction. Some weaknesses in a deal can be resolved by improving governance rights; others might need part of the investment structure to change—for example, changing the perimeter of assets to be acquired or financed to make for a better deal.

At today's investment committee meeting at the Firm, two contrasting opportunities are under consideration: They are different in sector, geography, and risk/return—but similar in terms of how the Firm approaches them. Over the course of three hours, the committee debates searing questions in a dynamic dialog designed to peel back each of the proposed deals to their most truthful essence—and to try to put investors' money to work. Let's put ourselves in the boardroom to witness these billions of dollars on the move.

"We're not bailing him out. We're taking the lead."

The deal partner on the complex mess known as Project Rubik acknowledges at the outset of the investment committee discussion the possibility of negative optics. He's attempting to clarify how he thinks the proposed investment should be seen, both internally and by the market. Yes, it is a hairy situation: The seller is a crumbling and controversial empire, owned by a scandal-prone industrialist family in Asia, but the deal itself is the straightforward purchase of a healthy, desirable asset. In fact, there is the potential for the Firm to emerge from the mess and be seen as one of the few buyers in the world capable of sorting out the situation. It could end up looking like a smart bargain for a savvy buyer.

The seller is Raptor Industries Limited, a privately held conglomerate headquartered in Asia that until recently had multinational interests in mobile phones, petroleum extraction and refining, and corporate banking. Two of the three verticals are now gone, with the telecom division sold for a handsome profit to a U.S. competitor, and the financial services division temporarily shut down by regulators while a tax and accounting scandal is being investigated. Believing that they had something of a Midas touch, the founding family had invested the four billion dollars received from the telecom sale into a string of impressive failures, in sectors ranging from infrastructure to private aviation, and it is these missteps and the debt attached to them that now loom over the group, starving it of the cash it needs to pay interest costs, salaries, and suppliers. The once-mighty conglomerate now consists of the energy division, a profitable business, and this string of failed assets. The situation is a case of bad luck colluding with poor judgment. Just the kind of thing that catches private equity's eye.

With the seller in trouble, the family's net worth is not more than a fifth of its former peak. The conglomerate has borrowed at every level, filling up each pocket available with leverage, and has given out company pledges over most of its assets—and personal guarantees, just like ordinary folks often do when taking out debt. Now, the lending banks have forced the sale of the family's trophy assets as part of a deleveraging plan for the conglomerate. Out goes the five-story townhouse on the Upper East Side, the Gulfstream private jet, and the one-hundred-foot yacht moored off the South of France. But even with these proceeds, most of the outstanding debt remains. The lending banks hire Wall Street firms to explore what they can do with the pledges they hold over the teetering empire's energy division: deep water oil fields, oil storage tanks and pipelines, and a refining facility specialized in processing unleaded gasoline and bioethanol. Surely, plenty of cash can be wrung out of them to repay the loans that soon will come due.

Raptor's energy assets are large enough to rule out all but the largest, most sophisticated buyers but too small to be of scale to survive long-term in a decarbonizing world. The oil majors would rather the energy division die in the family's hands than spend their shareholders' money on a purchase that might attract the attention of the antitrust authorities. When Wall Street bankers call them, they show little interest, asking only for a last look if other bidders fail to materialize.

The irony is that, of all the family's businesses, the energy division is healthy and well run. It has been the source of the family's industrial reputation for twenty years, and it will not be given up without a vicious fight. The family balks at the lending banks' talk of selling the energy division to private equity, and they are upset that the Wall Street firms hired by the lending banks have already called the major firms to explore a buyout. The family is desperate to retain control of their prize asset.

But as the parties head toward a stalemate, one of the senior family members reaches out to the Firm's deal partner on Rubik—the same guy who bought the family's Manhattan brownstone and kept his promise not to reveal to the media how much of a terrific bargain he got for five thousand square feet of ultra-prime real estate.

Away from the glaring eyes of Wall Street, the deal partner

and his team have secured an edge: They have been privately debriefed by the family for the past three weeks on every nook and cranny of Raptor's finances, meeting in unimposing office space far from the Midtown skyscrapers that private equity firms call home. The family knows that the Firm is unlikely to be interested in a broad auction of the energy division where the winner is the highest bidder, and the Firm knows that the family is not at liberty (or keen) to strike a deal below market. The deal team must be creative if they have any hope of aligning the stars—including the fair demands of the creditors to the conglomerate.

Emerging from these brainstorming sessions with the family is an idea—one that the deal partner on Rubik is now proposing to the investment committee. The energy division needs capital to grow, to be able to acquire small assets and scale itself to be of potential interest to the oil majors or to the stock market for a public listing, when the time to exit draws near. For the moment, it needs to stay intact and to grow from a position of strength without getting distracted by the noise of debt crises at the conglomerate level. The partner proposes a buyout, with additional investment money earmarked for expansion as part of the business plan to be agreed on with the management team. Two billion dollars for the target and five hundred million more for tuck-in acquisitions and organic initiatives such as new facilities for storage, a budget for further exploration, and optimizing the configuration of the refinery to boost profitable output. The purchase price is reasonable, neither high nor low; in short, it is the right price for the business without the buyer's premium that would likely result from a competitive auction.

But what really stacks the deck is the deal team's credit solution. The partner proposes that the Firm's credit fund extend a private debt package to the lending banks to refinance their struggling loans, at a modest ten percent discount to par value. The credit fund will bypass the banking market entirely and lend directly to the group under a single umbrella facility known as a "unitranche." This new facility combines two and a half billion dollars of senior and junior level debt into a single shot. All the banks must do is accept a bit of pain, write off the remaining ten percent of what they are owed—and then they can get their money back within weeks. They will also get full proceeds from the sale of the energy division to the Firm's private equity fund. In other words, rather than just coming to the family's rescue, private equity has, in a sense, come to the banks' rescue. The world of debt recovery at this scale involves costly, protracted lawsuits—and can burn relationships. The Firm is stepping in to take the lead, sort out the mess, acquire the prize asset, and allow the banks a nearly full recovery, counting the interest they have earned as well as the principal they would recoup from their rapid exit. The Firm is acting as a lender through the unitranche, a lender that also has expertise in and might not mind taking over the borrower if the situation were to arise—for example, if the group cannot repay the debt or adhere to the agreed covenants with the credit fund. And these covenants are strict, as one might expect from the Firm.

The plan is audacious and comprehensive. For the lending banks, who did not see such a bold proposal coming, it is also irresistible. Here is a buyer with a multilayered answer to Raptor's problems, itself a major existing client of many of the lenders, with ample firepower to invest and a track record of swift execution. The family's support is part of the package, and by disintermediating Wall Street and striking a deal directly, the banks can save themselves perhaps a hundred million dollars in refinancing and advisory fees. That the Firm will charge a one-time fee of ten million dollars for arranging the deal amounts to a rounding error. It seems straightforward for the banks to cancel the pledges and personal guarantees that remain. The pragmatic move is to accept the offer and move on.

For the family, the transaction gives them breathing room to make something good from the ventures they invested in rather than losing them in a bitter fight. They were always going to have to sell the energy division anyway; better, then, to do so to the private equity affiliate of their new creditor than to a buyer they would likely never see again. As a deal sweetener, they also graciously accept a tiny stake of five percent in the energy division in return for a five-year advisory agreement to assist the Firm in its plans for the unit. They become part of the experts on the energy division's board of directors. They're now part of the Firm's library of people and data.

Of course, like the project's namesake, Rubik, the Firm's strategy for this investment involves more than a single move to achieve a winning outcome. The committee knows that what the partner is putting forward is just the start. Once complete, there are several levers to pull and dials to turn—multiple pathways to create value.

For the energy division, following a few years of revenue growth and cost slimming, the assets can be dissected into neat parcels for different types of investors—the upstream fields to investors willing to risk capital on discovering reserves and developing known wells; the storage facilities and petroleum pipelines to infrastructure investors looking for hard physical assets with long-term contracted revenues, a stable forward order book from customers, and predictable capital expenditure; and the refinery to specialist energy investors comfortable with the cyclical nature of refining margins and its working capital needs.

Some of the bidders for these assets might be other parts of the Firm; the Firm's infrastructure fund could, with the special permission of its investors, acquire the storage and pipelines, for example. It's been done before, and no doubt it will happen again. Trading assets within a firm's web of affiliated funds might even become a "new normal" for complex deals such as these— with investor oversight, of course.

The deal partner provides this commentary to the investment committee. The deal team then reviews the rest of the project's details, including the financial returns, the due diligence risks and possible mitigations, the target's management team, and candidates for the board. At the end of the presentation of the opportunity to the investment committee, the deal partner summarizes the holistic approach he intends for the Firm to adopt with a tongue-in-cheek remark.

"Trust me. Nothing good will be left to waste."

His colleagues break into knowing smiles and then begin the cross-examination. Having digested the materials, the group is prepared with a healthy mix of questions about the sector, business, management, financing, the counterparties—and the path to a lucrative exit. The process—the interrogation—is not for the faint of heart.

Why do these assets need to exist? What drives supply, demand, and competition? What is the oil price deck that underpins this thesis? What is the band of outcomes for returns? Why are refining margins forecast to increase? What are the economics of storage? Why is the cash flow predicted to jump in year two? Why are we backing this CEO? How can we finance working capital needs more efficiently? How can we reconfigure the refinery for a higher gross margin? How are we going to reconfigure the cost base? How can we be confident of the earnings peaks and troughs we are modeling? Which executives do we need to upgrade and why? Will there be damaging strikes? Who is going to eventually buy the asset, and at what valuation range? Explain Plan B—what happens if we are stuck with this asset for longer than we'd like? Can we extract cash dividends? What is the strategy to sell down the debt? Where are the scenarios for a recession or a pandemic?

It takes two hours to progress through pages of answers to questions that were anticipated, and discuss the questions that were not. Thick packs of Excel exhibits containing the relevant supporting analysis to most of the questions asked already sit atop the boardroom table. They are double-stapled and have sticky notes highlighting the key numbers and analyses. Every single pack is soon in use. Every person is an active participant. Every query is designed to test the judgment of the deal team. The investment committee notes the absence of support from governments, the presence of unions, the possibility of regulatory intervention, and the reaction of competitors to an investment by private equity. The views of Wall Street financing banks, management consultants, and operating advisors drawn from industry are thrown in. If there are big weaknesses in the thesis or business plan, it's likely that they will be revealed through the discussion. And the deal team will be the first to admit it. They want maximum buy-in, not narrow approval. If the deal goes wrong down the line, it should be a shock to *everyone*.

Eventually, there is consensus around the table. Terms are tweaked, tactics are refined, the permutations of the Rubik's Cube are assessed, and the investment committee and finally the Founder himself give the green light to proceed. It's a thrilling, exhausting, typical outcome. And the beginning of at least five years of work.

The project demonstrates the power of the Firm's franchise, and the Founder loves it. Of course, there will be tweaks and perhaps even a few material changes, but overall this is the kind of big-ticket solution that he has long envisaged. Multiple funds, with distinct needs but common goals—to find large, compelling situations where the Firm's industry knowledge, large fund sizes, analytical rigor, and network access make the difference. Taken together across private equity and credit, the Firm plans to commit five billion dollars. There are fewer than ten rivals on the planet that could dream of pulling this off.

The Founder signals a short break to change the subject, and asks the Human Resources team to brief the group about progress made in efforts related to diversity, climate change, and community impact. In the past six months, six press releases have been issued on these subjects. This is double the amount of the previous year and six times the number of five years ago.

The Firm has evolved; it's now a multi-billion-dollar public company managing hundreds of billions of dollars of investors' money across investment strategies. It's giving back a lot more to society: education grants to local community colleges; affirmative action programs for hiring and education; home office setups for employees; plans to hire veterans in portfolio companies; refurbishment of local parks and community sports facilities; and a "Dragon's Den" style contest for entrepreneurial ideas—for the youngest, newest employees. It's a far cry from the stereotypical image of excess often heard on Wall Street about private equity. In fact, it's closer to the image of a responsible anchor of the economy, an industrial stalwart.

One of the partners then reviews the joint ventures and minority investments the Firm has made in areas not typically covered by the funds' traditional activities. Blockchain technology start-ups, financial technology, social housing, wind turbines, student loans, and new medicines. The Firm's franchise is powerful enough to strike a deal in any part of the economy, and these are all new fields for the Firm to tap into.

The partner goes on to review the media coverage the Firm has courted for all of these initiatives. A number of the senior partners are on TV more often, and they attend more conferences and speak publicly. Slowly but surely, the Firm, like its rivals, is assuming the public role of a major actor in the economy thanks to this kind of media exposure. The Founder embraces the revised approach, including social media, for it makes the Firm look more in touch. And it means that casual observers pay more attention to the Firm's investment successes, and to the health and growth of the Firm, than to the more sensitive topics of high compensation or low tax rates that the media otherwise have tended to focus on. By engaging with the media, the Firm lays out a positive story proactively. It's a long way from the days when the Firm, seeking to cultivate an air of mystery, avoided the press almost entirely.

Once the group refocuses after this interlude, the investment committee's attention turns to the second deal on the agenda. The project is ordered last, because having read the materials sent by the team in advance, the partners assessed that it would be the quicker of the two deals to reach an answer on. The deal partner provides an express commentary on the situation, outlining the returns and the risks plus the key numbers, and opens the floor for questions. He can guess where the conversation will soon head, and so he does not ask for specific approvals. Rather, he suggests a direction that the Firm could take and invites his colleagues to probe.

The Founder kicks the discussion off with a rhetorical question: "Have we captured the pen stroke risk?" This refers to the possibility that a change in government regulations—executed via the "stroke of a pen"—can radically change the parameters of an investment.

The target is the largest operator of nursing homes in Western Europe, Lifetrust Corp. Started in 1980 as the brainchild of an immigrant entrepreneur from India who had noticed traditional attitudes to caring for elderly parents changing rapidly in his own community, Lifetrust dominates the market in five large European economies and has a toehold in five more in Southern and Eastern Europe. Its services are expensive, but standards are high and there is a relentless focus on safety. The next stage of Lifetrust's growth requires an investment of three hundred million dollars, and so with the aid of Wall Street banks, Lifetrust had struck a deal to accept an equity injection from the largest Asia-based private equity fund at a premium valuation. This fund, which has its headquarters in China, has a reputation for paying top dollar for deals they believe in, but from time to time they seem to end up badly overpaying for one reason or another. The Asian fund's investment was completed just before the start of the Covid-19 pandemic.

The problem with this investment is that the revenue streams are highly dependent on the level of government subsidies given to families to be able to afford the care that Lifetrust provides at premium prices. Long spells of care in the company's facilities are too expensive for most families, and so the company has gotten used to receiving generous state subsidies in each of its markets that top up what the families pay as clients. The company is comfortable with this reliance, because it is still cheaper for taxpayers to fund private operators than to pay governments to build and run public facilities to look after the elderly and others in need of specialist care. Lifetrust has not had any scandals, the facilities are well run, and the employees genuinely care about their patients, who they recognize are their clients as well as their responsibility. As long as the subsidies continue, the ecosystem should be stable, and a win-win for families, governments, and the company.

What the Asian fund has now realized, however, is that, owing to the Covid-19 pandemic, the level of subsidies has not kept up with the soaring costs of caring for vulnerable, healthcare-dependent patients—and this gap is growing. Public sector finances are stretched, and although the subsidies will not likely decrease, the cost inflation experienced by the company is steadily eating into profits. In fact, private equity ownership of the assets may become an issue, because there is little political appetite to provide more support to a private equity fund's investment from state coffers. Raising prices will not work, because families are already paying what they can afford. Staff are in short supply, and there are few costs that can be trimmed without compromising the quality of service being provided. The expected investment returns from the deal are starting to look low, like those for a public utility—half of what had been expected.

And what's more, the situation may get worse. There is talk in political circles of a regulated cap on prices or, at the very least, a mandatory rise in minimum investment thresholds in the facilities. The direction of public policy is headed toward greater supervision of the industry, setting out guidelines for the economics—or worse, direct regulation. This is scary, uncharted territory.

It is in this context that the Asian fund has turned to the Firm to sell down half its interest in the company, a year into the Covid-19 pandemic. Their hope is that a private equity powerhouse with experience in healthcare investments could bring fresh ideas to create value, and its contacts in government and among the regulators could be useful to explain the situation and get at least some measure of further state support. The acquisition debt loaded onto the company's books consists of private loans held by Chinese banks, which are unlikely to sell or refinance them at a discount, or at all. There is no credit angle for the Firm to consider. So too with the real estate sitting underneath the nursing homes; the land is leased, so there is no property angle—for example a sale and leaseback transaction. The deal is clear and straightforward: Buy half the business for a lower valuation than the Asian fund paid, reflecting the risks, or walk. Half the board seats and half the influence. A fifty-fifty split. The Firm would draw on its healthcare investment franchise to make something good of the situation, with a better exit outcome for both investors, but perhaps over a longer time frame than the Asian fund had first expected.

The Founder's question cuts to the heart of the proposition and is more relevant than price. Even at a lower valuation than the Asian fund paid, the investment relies on an evolving set of risks that, although possible to model as different scenarios, are difficult to assign reasonable probabilities to. The Firm does not gamble on which case might be right or blend probable outcomes, and it has little interest in unprincipled bets. True, other private equity firms might take a different view—good firms, which have made a success of situations such as this—but for the Founder and the industry giant he leads, the situation has far too many unknowns.

The deal partner has wisely suggested the Firm do more work, check its numbers, and stay engaged, knowing that for now, this is the best way forward. It might be that the right thing to do is just learn, and then, in the event that the company implodes, return later to reexamine the art of the possible. It might also be that the project ends up serving as little more than a learning experience for the Firm to start up a business in this or an adjacent sector at some point in the future.

For now, there is no chance to stack the deck, to generate favorable odds, to create an edge. And so, the right answer is to focus on investments where the situation has a better story, even if it's more complex. Every dollar has an opportunity cost—and there is too much risk in exchange for an uncertain return. They agree to review the Lifetrust situation in two weeks.

As the investment committee meeting draws to a close, one of the private equity partners reflects on how the Firm seems to be doing a deal a month these days, outpacing even the biggest and best-funded of acquisitive public corporations. Every year, billions of dollars are deployed and raised—in some years tens of billions of dollars. The Firm seems to be on track to achieve its goal of managing a trillion dollars of investors' money. The Founder looks at his partner, smiles, and offers a clarifying remark that serves as a warning not to get carried away and to focus on their mission.

"I don't worry about reaching a trillion. Let's concentrate on our work, and growth and size will follow. If there's one thing I can't stand, it's greed."

\*    \*    \*

In the next chapter, we envisage the sum total of what private equity can bring to an investment, accounting for the principles and facets we have explored, including the relentless drive to win and the library. We look at a situation that could well happen someday to illustrate the immense power of the major private equity firms. The sketch involved is based on a situation rooted in real experience, albeit scaled up. In this scenario, a private equity firm turns its analytical lens on a competitor. The target for private equity is not a company or a loan but a rival investment firm in trouble.

# CHAPTER THIRTEEN

# The Edge

"They failed to evolve."

These four words from the deal partner in the investment committee serve as a cutting indictment of one of the Firm's rivals. Madison Stone was established during meetings at the Four Seasons hotel on East 57th Street in Manhattan in the same year that the Founder left a leading investment bank on Wall Street to set up the Firm. But unlike the Firm, Madison Stone still looks much like it always has, despite its outward success over the last thirty years. It only invests in leveraged buyouts, it has not ventured much overseas, and it is reliant on a narrow set of U.S. pension funds for capital commitments. Madison Stone's founders look a little like portraits from a 1990s movie about Wall Street, and although they genuinely care about greater diversity in their ranks, just ten percent of the partners are non-white. The offices are quiet and formal; it is the kind of place that exudes an air of fabulous wealth but sometimes puts off young, hungry interview candidates, who find the atmosphere stifling and old-fashioned.

Madison Stone's partners take off on Friday afternoons for the Hamptons, usually flying by helicopter, and are back late Sunday to touch base with their deal teams. If urgent projects call for weekend dialog, calls are set before 9 A.M. Eastern on Saturday so as to limit the intrusion into personal downtime. FedEx parcels transmit investment memos and printouts of Excel financial models ahead of the deal discussions on Monday morning. The firm encourages participation in athletic pursuits and offers generous fitness programs. Twice a year, the firm hosts three-day team-building events: once at Aspen to ski and once in the Caribbean for a beach break. Holiday presents and birthday cakes for employees are never missed. Madison Stone is a good place to work, and the staff is very gracious.

But now, after decades as an industry stalwart—perhaps the most stable and recognized brand in the business—the firm faces a once-unthinkable challenge. A special committee of the private equity firm's largest investors has called for Madison Stone's funds to be managed by a third party. In other words, their *passive* investors want regime change. The pension funds are surprised by, and sick of, the unexpected infighting among the leadership of Madison Stone. Even worse, they are shocked by the sudden, sharp dip in the investment performance of the firm's funds. One of the funds' largest and most public leveraged buyouts has gone bust, an outcome that the pension funds justifiably believe better oversight and teamwork could have avoided.

The tipping point came six months earlier, when the original chemistry among Madison Stone's three founding partners started to falter. The triumvirate are cousins, each in their sixties, as well as co-owners. They live in a tight triangle between the Upper East Side, Midtown, and Central Park and were once held up as the model for how to maintain a rock-solid professional bond in a notoriously demanding industry.

All of that collapsed over the thorny issue of succession, when one member of the aging trio refused to change the "key

employee" provisions in Madison Stone's fund agreements with
its investors. These provisions specify the most important people
at the firm, individuals without whom the business might not be
able to function at all. The provisions recognize the reliance of
the investors on a handful of individuals—no matter how large
and established the organization—and in Madison Stone's case,
they were due to be updated with new names in addition to the
three founders, to reflect the senior partners who were in line
to be handed the reins within three years. One of the founders
had other ideas and said he was not ready to set his retirement
plans just yet.

The firm's partnership was aghast at his obstinance, and
within twelve weeks, all of Madison Stone's brightest stars had
left to join rivals or start their own firms. They didn't mind the
lengthy non-compete clauses or the temporary hit on their
compensation—each partner was worth over a hundred million
dollars. They resented the glass ceiling, and they wanted out.

The talent crater widened, as top investment professionals
at competing firms, repelled by the negative internal dynam-
ics at Madison Stone, declined headhunters' calls to consider
moving there. Inevitably, the funds' investment performance
dropped markedly. As the prognosis worsened, the funds' investors invoked an emergency clause in the fund agreements to call
a vote to replace Madison Stone as the manager of their money,
citing its inability to function effectively, and in a late-night
emergency session overseen by counsel, the investors agreed to
remove the firm once a more suitable active asset manager could
be found to manage the assets already acquired by the firm's
funds (and eventually to sell them off for a profit, a situation
known as a "run-off" of the portfolio). What was once a positive
dynamic among the top people at Madison Stone, which gener-

ated strong investment returns for decades, had been reduced to a negative dynamic that would lead to the firm's effective demise.

The founders of Madison Stone accepted their fate, though they were adamant that none of the firm's industry peers should take over—but, of course, the decision was not theirs to make. They could only watch.

At this juncture, a representative of the investors' special committee calls a deal partner at the Firm to pitch for the role. The partner can't help but smile as he takes in the request. The way the special committee representative describes Madison Stone even makes the partner chuckle. What a mess they are in, the partner muses. The special committee believes that the Firm is one of a handful of suitable candidates to run off Madison Stone's funds. The partner agrees to revert after consulting with the Firm's investment committee. The Firm decides to pitch for the role.

Ten days later, the partner meets with the special committee to provide a comparison between the Firm's trajectory over the past thirty years and that of Madison Stone. It is clear to the special committee that although the two firms were founded in the same year, the Firm is light-years ahead. It has grown to be more than three times larger than Madison Stone in assets under management across its investment strategies for private capital. The Firm has the best tools and people in data science, information technology, financial reporting, risk management, and environmental impact—part of the core infrastructure of a modern private equity firm. The Firm already has a preliminary view on each asset in Madison Stone's portfolio, using its library—of the macro picture and the micro trends of the customers, suppliers, and supply and demand. The Firm has data mining executives on tap to assist each company in Madison Stone's portfolio with benchmarking the key operating numbers that drive revenues, cost, capital expenditure, and cash flow. It has positions in debt, infrastructure, real estate, and commodities investments in businesses that populate the ecosystems of Madison Stone's portfolio. It's like the Firm has a sixth sense, a dimension of insight beyond what Madison Stone can offer.

Not to mention billions of dollars of available capital through the Firm's funds to help Madison Stone's portfolio companies grow organically and complete acquisitions, if that were to make sense. To supersize, in short. The Firm is of a different scale from Madison Stone.

On top of this, the partner continues, the Firm has taken many steps forward as an organization. Succession planning is set for the next decade, with the next layers of management in place. The "key employee" provisions were updated, without infighting. Where Madison Stone failed, the Firm has succeeded. This speaks to the cohesion inside the Firm, and its leadership.

When the partner is done talking, it is clear to the special committee that the Firm has progressed from a one-trick pony doing private equity to a vast, multi-strategy investment powerhouse. And its stock is listed on the New York Stock Exchange, pushing through more transparency at the Firm and adding layers of regulation and oversight that a private partnership like Madison Stone does not have. The special committee is impressed and promises to revert to the Firm within two weeks.

When the call from the special committee comes to negotiate the terms under which the Firm would replace Madison Stone, the partner seeks approval from the investment committee to finalize an arrangement. He asks for latitude to negotiate the final terms, within defined bounds, as he wants to be able to conclude matters quickly.

Enthusiastic about the idea, the Founder is convinced that his investment professionals can create more value out of the portfolio than Madison Stone. The numbers back up his optimism: Even in reasonable downside cases or scenarios where the investments must be held longer than expected, the investment returns more than compensate investors for the risks taken. Given that the idea has broad support, the partner spends a few minutes discussing the two largest investments in the Madison Stone portfolio and what can be done in the near term to improve them.

The first business is a large discount retailer with stores in major cities across America and in Europe. Every item for sale in each store retails at less than a dollar or euro, depending on the location. Madison Stone's private equity fund had acquired a majority stake in the company from the retailer's founding family, which had organized funding rounds from venture capital firms but then looked for private equity shareholders to inject additional capital to grow the footprint and help broaden the product range. Madison Stone placed the highest bid in an auction run by Wall Street banks on behalf of the retailer, took control, and started to scout for sites and assist the management with the ambitious growth plans.

Everything went well for the first twenty-four months. But when Madison Stone's internal squabbles stole the deal team's focus away from the investment, missteps followed. Changes in sales tax rates impacted the pricing strategy and profit margins in some of the most important markets for the business, as governments increased their cut of every dollar earned by the company. The retailer required urgent attention from its owner to revamp pricing, cut costs, and form closer links with regulators. Madison Stone attended one working group meeting out of every four they were invited to, often sending first-year juniors instead of seasoned professionals. The deal team's partner attended only high-level board meetings, where all the action was in the rear-view mirror. He became a spectator, rather than the athlete he was trained and hired to be. His mind was elsewhere.

Decisions made by a good management team were delayed, fresh investment in rebranding and relationships with suppliers stalled, visits to the European operations dried up, and within four quarters the financial picture was looking far worse than a temporary blip. Most alarming of all for investors, there was no way out of the mess with Madison Stone still in charge. The enterprise needed a present, engaged investment firm to apply the pressure and assistance that private equity ownership is known for. This was precisely the kind of support that the Firm would be keen and fit to provide.

What edge does the Firm have? The Firm's funds have not owned a discount retailer before. But the funds have just invested in a budget food retail chain, a kitchen appliance sup-plier, and a major operator of kiosks and convenience stores. The Firm's deal team has worked with smart management teams in each situation to identify the right retail sites or to negotiate distribution contracts and supply agreements or to consider the impact of sales taxes. The Firm's network is deep and broad in retail, and, following a detailed search by headhunters, it can access strong candidates for executive management and board roles as required. Another pocket of the Firm, one of the real estate funds, has investments in the type of commercial spaces where budget retail groups lease their stores. No information is shared inappropriately between the real estate funds and the private equity fund, of course. But overall, the Firm's profession-als have absorbed a high level of general knowledge about these dimensions, including market cycles, rental rates, and pressures and opportunities in retail. The Firm isn't invested in the same space as the target, but it's involved in relevant neighboring ecosystems.

The second company in the Madison Stone portfolio is the largest operator of parking lots in Europe. Founded after World War II by a young entrepreneur who bought up bomb shelters and disused warehouses, the business has prime sites in the center of major cities where customers pay premium prices for convenient and safe spots. Although the business had been in private equity hands twice before Madison Stone acquired it, the management team was keen to take the business to the next level. Their idea was to expand in emerging markets based on strong car ownership forecasts and a growing appetite for more expensive vehicles. The thesis sold to Madison Stone made sense: bigger markets for premium cars and more folks keen to park them in safe, spacious places. The capital expenditure invested in emerging markets worked out well, but what caught Madison Stone off-guard was the sudden erosion of demand in the core, mature markets.

The rise of Uber and its peers; escalating car ownership costs, including fuel and insurance; and higher rental charges for leased sites all led cash flow to weaken precisely as overseas expansion required more cash to fund it. Madison Stone was distracted; the deal partner, too focused on the cut and thrust of internal firm politics, soon resigned as part of the frustrated senior group who felt disenfranchised by the firm.

As with the discount retailer, what the parking operator craved, and lacked, was attention from its private equity owner and the symbiotic working relationship between private equity and management. Introducing the Firm would not be a quick fix but could instead be an effective solution to guide the asset to a lucrative exit. A good business, a rough spot, and a deteriorating cash flow and balance sheet add up to a great opportunity.

What edge does the Firm have? Here, the Firm's deal partner had previously bid for the company in a competitive auction to buy it, losing out to Madison Stone. He returned the information from the auction, of course, but he still remembers how to look at the sector and this asset. It's not like he can just forget, nor should he try. As the losing bidder the first time, he is all the more credible the second time around. The Firm, having also financed the rollout of charge points for electric cars through a private credit facility to a successful start-up in this emerging field, has a good handle on likely ownership and usage trends across fuel platforms. Perhaps part of the parking lots can be used to charge electric cars. Taken together, the deal partner has a superior information set than other candidates will bring to the table.

As it analyzes Madison Stone's holdings, members of the Firm's investment committee note that the Firm would not be the first outside fund manager to attempt changing the fate of Madison Stone's portfolio. Even before the special committee ousted Madison Stone from control, the largest single debt investor to many of the businesses in the portfolio had grown increasingly concerned about the assets' worsening quarterly results and forecasts. This debt investor, a credit fund that is part of a major specialized credit investment firm, felt that without course correction from Madison Stone, many of the assets in the portfolio were creeping toward breaching their debt covenants. Proactively, they offered to help, suggesting that some of their own restructuring experts could run a slide rule over the businesses that needed attention. The reply from Madison

Stone was a reluctant yes, knowing their own resources were thinly stretched.

The help didn't change anything. Sure, the new resources from the debt investor added more analysis to what Madison Stone had run. But what was missing from the portfolio companies was not analysis but investment experience. Madison Stone needed operating and financing know-how from private equity executives accustomed to working with management, not more Excel models to diagnose problems they were mostly aware of.

The Firm's partners debate whether their deal partner is being too optimistic, and whether it would be smarter to wait for the assets to crash and then step in to salvage the remains. They agree that it would be better to take over management of the assets now—better for the investors in the funds and better for the Firm in terms of the fees and profit share that it would be eligible for if the assets are exited successfully at Two and Twenty.

The investment committee decides to enrich the economics of the arrangement a little, to compensate for the risks that cannot be resolved adequately in due diligence—for example, the possibility that the rot in certain companies is worse than the data suggests or that the workforces in other businesses are less cooperative than might be reasonable to expect. The best shield against these issues is to make the terms sweeter for the Firm.

The Firm is positioned as a "white knight" to the special committee, and within three months, Madison Stone is replaced. For the deal partner, the project carries a touch of personal amusement as well as a professional interest. Twenty years ago, when he completed a two-year financial analyst program at Merrill Lynch, he interviewed at Madison Stone as his top choice in the private equity industry. It was the place to be. After twelve interviews, he was rejected. The feedback from the firm's Human Resources team was that he lacked the creativity they were looking for.

As his deal team gathers in his office to discuss starting work on the project under the new engagement from the special committee, the partner muses that, in the intervening two decades, he and his peers at the Firm have learned to be far more creative than Madison Stone, a firm that has failed to innovate and adapt. He whispers loud enough for the deal team to hear.

"They're just a private equity firm. We're the Eighth Wonder of the World."

From the outside looking in, it can be tempting to think of all private equity firms as pretty much identical, with similar ways of making money for investors. In reality, nothing could be further from the truth in the industry today. The best private equity firms can boast not only *edge* but *evolution*. The major firms have realized that just doing one thing—even at greater scale—is not going to keep them winning on deals, growing assets under management, or cementing their relationships with investors. It might work for a while, but the competitive pressures of the industry mean that to win, you have to have more to your game. Certainly, staying a one-trick firm will not likely build the brand value and scale needed to either go public or, if already public, to propel the stock price further and broaden the share ownership base and get the ticker included in the major indices.

And so, regardless of how they started—whether leveraged buyout shops or distressed debt shops or sector-specific shops focused on technology or natural resources, for example—the best firms have evolved to be capable of handling a broad range of incoming investment ideas while keeping their workforces compact relative to the enormous size of the asset piles they manage. From the project mentioned in this sketch to any of the sketches mentioned in previous chapters, they are able to handle it all with dispassionate analysis and rational debate about the risk/return trade-offs. They're capable of having an answer to nearly everything.

They have achieved this evolution, remarkably, without diluting the cultures and working practices that are specific to their firms and the traits of success we have been discussing. Lateral hires have been integrated into partnerships and senior management layers, and first-class talent has been brought in to run key parts of a firm's infrastructure from the CFO's office to human capital to data science. Where it has made sense to seed or buy a stake in another firm rather than start up a new industry vertical, they have taken the opportunity to do so. Double-digit growth, delivered each year.

Whisper it softly . . . but the truth is that comparing what private equity firms used to be—and where the perception of private equity still sits in many quarters—to what they are now is like comparing a Motorola cellphone from the 1990s to the latest iPhone. There's a world of differences; it's not even close. For pension funds and other investors in private equity funds, the firms they back gives them access to investment opportunities they can't find or execute themselves. What's more, they get consistent investment returns out of these opportunities, whether they include leveraged buyouts, credit investments, infrastructure assets, essential utilities, real estate transactions, technology deals, natural resources projects, banks, insurance companies, or life science opportunities. They can buy companies, carve out businesses, build up companies through acquisitions and organic growth, spin off businesses, take companies private from the public market, buy businesses from other funds they manage, draw margin loans to finance dividends, and refinance the capital structure pre-exit. And more besides.

The new edge is versatility.

And what goes hand in hand with versatility is scale.

When we zoom out a little from the day-to-day picture of what private equity does, we can see this versatility edge more clearly and start to question whether we can still call these investment firms "alternative."

It is true that private capital, including private equity, remains smaller than the passive asset management industry, where the fees are much lower (for example, ten basis points per year in ETF vehicles—if that—versus Two and Twenty) and the vehicles generally track major market indices. But it is now a little outdated to label these firms "alternative."

Think of it this way: The largest publicly listed firms are collectively worth over a quarter trillion dollars in market capitalization and together they manage over 2.5 trillion dollars of assets. They're the tip of the spear, with the rest of the industry—managing trillions of dollars more in assets—right behind. These aren't small niches.

The reality is that private equity has evolved so much that it is now *mainstream*. The leading firms are gigantic, mainstream, *active* asset managers of capital—much of it, ultimately, money belonging to retirees—across multiple investment strategies.

We even can coin a handy acronym, MAAM, to summarize them: Mainstream Active Asset Managers. These MAAM are led and run by relatively small sets of "key employees"—key individuals. Some firms have massive credit and lending businesses; some have major insurance entities; some manage prominent real estate investment funds. Alongside their private equity funds, there's a lot to like.

And unlike passive asset managers, the amount of capital flowing into these Mainstream Active Asset Managers is always booming year on year. Investors can't easily dip in and out. Private capital funds do not report the same market volatility as mutual funds and ETFs during periods of dislocation, such as the Covid-19 pandemic or the financial crisis, despite the swings in the asset values of their portfolios. They are patient, lock-up-and-leave boxes of capital. And they perform consistently using the traits we have discussed in this book. Thanks to this investment performance, the reliance of retirement systems and other investors on these masters of private equity—these individuals—will only increase. This is why the edge they have developed so well, to evolve, is also why, over time, these firms may be recognized not only as part of the mainstream in asset management and more broadly in financial services, but something profound in our economy—they could, one day, be considered to be *systemic.*

# The Age of Big Finance

"Are we adequately compensated for the risks that we're taking?"

This innocent-sounding question is perhaps the most funda-mental and striking line heard in the investment committee dur-ing deal discussions. It's a question you can't maneuver around. A line you can't ignore. A wrong answer or an incomplete answer, and you lose credibility. Try smoke and mirrors, and you're toast. I've witnessed both outcomes. Fortunately, far more frequently, I've seen balanced responses that are nuanced in argument and peppered with relevant data. And what results is billions of dol-lars of money from pension funds and other investors being put to work, multiplied, and returned—less, of course, Two and Twenty, or some variant of this formula, for fees.

The investments usually work out, and when they don't, the professionals involved have enormous incentives to put things right before it is too late. Not only for their careers, but also for the reputations of the firms they work for. In great private equity firms, you get credit for profitable exits, not just for put-ting someone else's money to work. The spotlight is harsh, and that is as it should be. When addressing the equation of risk versus return on a deal, there is, of course, some margin for error because the investment is usually private and you can hold the capital invested for longer if necessary to fix problems and restart momentum, but there is rarely much room for very serious miscalculation. You also don't really want to spend a decade of your life with your investors' money only to barely return it—or even worse, to lose it.

What if we were to turn this question on its head? What if the retirement systems and other investors in private equity were to ask this question of the private equity industry or, more broadly, of private capital? Are the expected returns worth it? Are we mis-pricing the risks? Do we agree with the work practices of private equity professionals and management teams, the level of transparency to investors, the degree of accountability, the influence over what is now a large and growing number of sizable operating businesses in important parts of the economy? What about the fees involved? Are they appropriate for the size of some funds in the industry today? Do we agree with the difference between returns before fees (gross returns) and returns after private equity's cut (net returns)? And do we understand the incentives at play? The interaction between management fees and carried interest? The interaction between a firm's stock price and its funds under management, and the investment performance of those funds? Or the social impact of the deals? Is there really any systemic risk?

These tough questions are not new for private equity. Neither are calls for tax rates on carried interest to match income tax rates—or at least for the spread between them to narrow. The same applies to calls for caps on the levels of high-yield debt that leveraged buyouts can rely on to enhance investment performance, calls for more transparency and greater accountability of private equity professionals when investments go wrong, calls for labor protections when private equity or indeed any form of private capital is involved in a business, calls for funding security for pension arrangements in private equity–backed companies, calls for regulators to restrict what private equity can and can't buy in one sector of the economy or another because the assets are deemed by regulators to be too "sensitive," and calls for regulators to supervise more closely the management of the firms.

Many of these questions have been in the mix for years and, despite feverish debate, they do not seem to show sign of clear resolution.

And plainly, when you read through some of the press that private equity firms get, plenty of misconceptions and misunderstandings about this industry are out there, alongside some very fair, if sometimes heated, questions. From the outside, it might be hard for observers to differentiate between signal and noise.

Debates about the merits of private equity can be polarizing— even weaponized. The scale of wealth created in the industry can tilt the discussion unfavorably in some circles. The critiques are well known: The industry creates too much wealth for too few at the top, the benefits to companies invested in are not always clear, the business model relies on too much debt, private equity is not a transparent industry, not enough is done for ordinary workers in private equity–backed deals, and so on. These points are not new, have been covered in the press, and occasionally gain political traction.

What is the way forward? Engagement. When you read adversarial comments on both sides, it becomes clear that it's time for cool heads and constructive speaking. Only greater understanding through engagement can lead the public to greater recognition that in our economy there is an important *symbiosis* between the investors who desire (or, in the case of pension funds, need) the returns that private equity generates, the firms who carry out the work and are rewarded for it, the companies that are invested in and the communities around these businesses, and, ultimately, the public. This doesn't mean that everyone has to like or agree with this interdependence. But it's key to recognize it and to acknowledge that it is already enormous and is growing fast. The ship that created this dynamic has sailed.

In my view, for the leading firms in particular, there has in recent years been serious and visible progress in big topics such as diversity, sustainability, and disclosure. It's also likely that as the firms continue to grow, the level of engagement will also grow as part of the flight path to invest, not only for institutions and high-net-worth families but also for the mass affluent market and, if regulators allow, for mom-and-pop retail investors. Private capital is too big to ignore.

More engagement would cast a favorable light on private equity and private capital, especially for the top firms. The private equity industry is now *mainstream*. More firms will manage over a hundred billion dollars each, and a handful will top a trillion dollars. With numbers this large, greater public understanding about private capital is not only likely but essential. It will be vital for individuals to understand what they are or might be exposed to in their pension schemes at least as much as they understand buying Amazon, Apple, or Alphabet, or any other stock in their own portfolios.

And as part of this public understanding, I think it's important to recognize that it is rare for private equity investments to fail and even rarer for private equity firms themselves to blow up—just look at how stable (and profitable) the sector has proven to be during the massive shocks of the financial crisis and the Covid-19 pandemic. The distributions made by private equity funds to investors are paid in cash, nearly always, made from realized gains or income from the investment—not from paper wealth. This happens year in, year out, through market cycles and the volatility of the public markets. Something must be going right for this to keep working.

Private capital is the new Big Finance. And with interest rates still low and parts of Wall Street firmly out of the spaces that private equity firms want to grow further in, the industry has room to be creative and grow its share of retirees' balance sheets by managing even larger slices of pension fund money.

This is *active* investing on a huge scale. Not market tracking, not index following. Private equity firms are always raising capital for one strategy or another, always deploying investors' money with one hand and returning cash back with the other. Their customers tend to commit to more than one fund and are increasingly sticky, usually returning for more. They have built high-growth businesses that are getting better every day. They're always winning.

The connective tissue running through this ecosystem is the *people* who lead and work in these firms. It's a people business, increasingly enabled by technology and data science, and it's the people, the masters of private equity, who make the active investment decisions that make the returns and earn Two and Twenty for it. It's their judgment that we are dependent on. That's why it's essential to better understand how they work, what drives them, and what influence they have on investments. That's what I have tried to shed some light on in these pages.

One way or another, we are all customers of private equity, whether in the form of buying goods and services from private capital–backed companies to investing in private capital through retirement systems or both. And I hope more people will realize that as we increasingly rely on this massive industry to ensure the financial security of our retirements and the financial security of our loved ones, more ordinary citizens will have a special interest in understanding how private capital really works, who does it well consistently, how we can benefit from it, where the industry is headed, and how we can contribute to a conversation about how to improve it.

We all need an active interest in private equity.

Why? Perhaps for one big reason, above all others.

Because we all have some skin in this fascinating game.

# Acknowledgments

I am grateful to my family for their support. My father is the inspiration for writing this book, and it is dedicated to him. Many friends, colleagues, and mentors in the industry shared valuable insights and perspectives, and I am indebted to them. My excellent agent, Eric Lupfer at Fletcher & Company, and my incredibly talented editor, Paul Whitlatch at the Crown imprint of Penguin Random House, believed in this book from the start. They offered positive feedback and wise counsel, and they were inquisitive and patient. This book would not be here without them. I would also like to thank the team at Penguin Random House, including Katie Berry, Evan Camfield, Cozetta Smith, Dyana Messina, Chantelle Walker, Julie Cepler, Chris Brand, Sally Franklin, Allie Fox, Michelle Giuseffi, David Drake, Gillian Blake, and Annsley Rosner.

# An Everyday Private Equity Glossary

The following terms are commonplace in the private equity industry and I use them in the book. The definitions are my own—written as plainly as possible, the way I would define them to a friend or a new co-worker.

**Alternative asset:** A specific type of asset that is less straight-forward to understand and to value than simpler assets like stocks and bonds. Alternative assets can be set up and actively managed by investment professionals at asset management firms. These assets can generate higher investment returns but can carry higher risk. Private capital and hedge funds are examples of alternative assets.

**Asset:** A store of value for investors, such as a financial asset (e.g., stock in a company or bonds that a company issues to raise money) bought or created with investors' money.

**Assets under management:** Investors' money that an asset management firm has under contract to manage. The money can be invested in alternative assets or in simpler assets, like stocks and bonds.

**Capital structure:** The specific combination of equity and debt used by a company or business to finance its operations and growth. The equity in the enterprise consists of the ownership rights and claims to future cash flow and profit. The debt is the money borrowed by the enterprise by issuing loans and bonds that are due to be paid back to lenders (usually with interest). If the enterprise goes bust, debt investors can usually try to get paid back what they are owed before equity investors can share in any value left over. Because debt investors are "owed back" first, they are considered to be "senior" to equity investors in the capital structure. Conversely, if the value of the enterprise rises, equity investors can share in this value increase, but debt investors ordinarily would not. In this sense, equity investors share in the "upside" of the enterprise.

**Cost structure:** The cost structure of a company defines the costs and expenses incurred (money spent) while running its business model. Typically, when looking at a potential investment in an enterprise, a private equity firm will look to take out any unnecessary cost and improve profitability, often known as "cutting the fat."

**Credit fund:** An investment fund set up by an asset management firm, such as a private equity firm, to invest in debt issued by companies or businesses, such as loans and bonds. The fund is managed by the investment professionals of the firm, and often the debt in which they invest is not accessible to investors directly. An example would be private loans that are arranged directly by the firm with companies or businesses who want to borrow money, or other loans that are not publicly traded. At some private equity firms, all investments in debt are carried out through credit funds. At other firms, the private equity fund can also invest in debt, often distressed debt, as well as carrying out leveraged buyouts and other forms of private equity investing.

**Creditor protections (including "covenants"):** A package of promises made by a borrower, such as a company or business that issues a bond or takes out a loan, for the benefit of creditors (the parties lending the money). The point of the promises is to protect creditors from the borrower defaulting on its obligation to pay back the debt and pay interest due (if any). The protection works through "covenants," or legally binding rules written in a formal debt agreement that restrict activities of the borrower that could be detrimental to creditors (e.g., restricting the amount of further debt that can be taken out, to keep debt within manageable levels, or selling key valuable parts of the enterprise without the permission of creditors). The covenants require that certain financial indicators be met or maintained (e.g., there must be enough room to cover interest expense from cash flow, or the total debt burden on the enterprise cannot exceed a certain multiple of its earnings). A breach of a covenant can trigger a right for creditors to demand their money back with any interest due.

**Crystallize (as in "to crystallize a gain"):** To monetize the change in value of an investment. For example, a private equity investment that has risen in value during its lifetime will have a financial gain associated with it, but until this gain is monetized into cash, it is only a theoretical gain on paper. Once the gain is turned into cash, it can be paid out to the investors.

**Deal team (and deal partner):** A team of investment professionals at a private equity firm or other asset management firm working on an investment opportunity. A deal team consists of a handful of individuals with varying levels of investment experience. Each individual can be a member of more than one deal team, and would likely work on more than one investment opportunity in parallel. The leader of a deal team is a partner—a senior investment professional at the firm who has reached the highest level of the ladder. Alternative titles for partners include Senior Managing Director or Member.

**Distressed debt:** Debt instruments, like loans and bonds, issued by companies or businesses that get into financial trouble. For example, perhaps after a period of weak financial results, the enterprise has failed to pay interest or, worse, to repay debt when it should have. The price of the debt will be at a steep discount to its face or "par" value—perhaps sixty or seventy cents on the dollar or less—because of the risk attached to an investment in a troubled enterprise. Often, the investment return that can be generated may be higher for distressed debt, to compensate investors for the higher risk they accept. A private equity fund may acquire distressed debt as an investment—for example, if it believes the enterprise will survive and is sound even though it is experiencing hard times temporarily.

**Draw down (as in "draw down a commitment"):** Money committed by investors to a private equity fund is not usually handed over to the private equity firm that manages the fund up front, because it is not invested immediately. Instead, the money is sent from investors over time as investments are made. Investors promise to send the money—documented in a legal agreement—and the fund issues a notice called a "capital call" when investors' money is needed to make investments. When the money is sent in this way from investors, the promise or commitment is being "drawn down."

**Dry powder:** The amount of unspent money available to a fund, such as a private equity fund. As investments are made, the amount of dry powder left in the fund decreases.

**Due diligence:** The work done by investment professionals and third-party advisors (e.g., accountants, tax specialists, management consultants, and lawyers) to assess the quality of a company or business being considered for investment and to critique the viability of the investment thesis.

**Edge [as in "having an edge" on a deal]:** An edge is a competitive strength or advantage for a bidder on a potential deal. The edge could be prior knowledge of the target company or business—or its competitors, or a good relationship with the owner of the target or its management team. The more substantial the edge, the more likely it is that the bidder may be able to secure the deal over rival bidders without overpaying for it.

**Entry:** The starting point of an investment—for example, when a company or business is acquired by a private equity fund. The fund has "entered" the investment at this point.

**Execution plan:** The work done by investment professionals to bridge from one stage of a deal to another, organized in a logical and systemic way. For example, moving from an idea for an investment to making the investment will require a plan for investigating the idea, testing the viability of the investment thesis (including due diligence), making an offer for the investment, and securing the deal. There will also be a long-term plan that covers the life cycle of an investment from start to finish, including steps for identifying whom to sell to. Investment professionals keep execution plans flexible to adapt to changing circumstances on a deal.

**Exit:** The end point of an investment—for example, when a company or business owned by a private equity fund is sold. The fund has "exited" the investment at this point.

**Governance rights [for example, for a private equity fund in an investment]:** The rights that the private equity fund will have over the company or business in which the investment is made. These rights can cover a number of topics, from the way decision-making is handled at the enterprise to the type of information about the enterprise to which the fund has access. For example, in a leveraged buyout in which an enterprise is acquired by a private equity fund, the fund will have the right to appoint some or all of the board of directors, including a chair, and likely the CEO too. The fund will also have the right to obtain financial and operating information from the enterprise in order to assess the progress and value of the investment. Typically, the level of governance rights an investor has matches the size and the materiality of its investment in the enterprise.

**Hedge fund:** An investment fund that typically trades in publicly traded and other liquid assets (rather than focusing on acquiring control of companies or businesses and holding them in a private fund, as a private equity fund does). A hedge fund investment is an example of an alternative asset, and hedge funds can use complex techniques to generate investment returns, such as the use of derivatives. They are not typically available to retail investors. Hedge funds can vary enormously in the types of investments they make, the level of risk they accept, and the return they expect to make to compensate for the risk. The Two and Twenty fee arrangement (and variations of it) found in the private equity industry is also common in the hedge fund industry.

**High-yield bond (also "high-yield debt"):** A bond issued by a company or business that has a comparatively high potential risk of a negative event, such as a failure to pay the interest due or pay back the money borrowed. To compensate investors for this risk, the bonds will have a higher interest rate.

**Index fund:** An investment fund that consists of a portfolio of simpler assets, like stocks, constructed to match or track a financial market index, like the S&P 500. The fund will follow the index regardless of changes in market conditions. Fees charged by index funds are much lower than for private capital funds because index funds passively follow an index. The idea is that in the long term, a broad and well-known index may outperform a small basket of stocks or a private capital fund.

**Investment bank:** A financial services organization that can act as an intermediary and an advisor in complex financial transactions. For example, an investment bank can raise money from investors for a growing company by underwriting the issuance of its equity or debt. An investment bank can provide financial advice to companies involved in mergers and acquisitions. Many investment banks also trade securities, such as equity, debt, and derivatives, and some may conduct other activities, such as asset management. When we talk about "Wall Street banks" in this book, we are talking about major investment banks such as Goldman Sachs and Morgan Stanley. These banks and their competitors advise private equity firms on buying, selling, and refinancing companies and businesses, and underwrite debt (for example, high-yield bonds) and equity (for example, IPOs) for these enterprises.

**Investment committee (in a private equity firm):** A decision-making body comprised of the partners of the firm—and the founder(s), if still at the firm—that meets regularly to approve or reject investment ideas, discuss progress on investments made, and review the performance of funds managed by the firm. Typically, all investment professionals at a firm (at all levels) are invited to and participate in investment committee meetings. At major firms, the investment committees meet often, such as once a week, with overseas offices dialing in to participate. For a private equity fund to be able to make an investment, the investment committee will first have had to approve it after discussing it.

**Investment memo:** A detailed piece of work on a prospective investment put together by investment professionals for discussion in the investment committee and other forums. A memo will usually contain financial analysis, discussion of the investment's strengths and weaknesses, and input from third-party advisors such as accountants, tax specialists, management consultants, and lawyers. The memo serves as the focal point for the investment committee discussion about the investment. Further memos are prepared once an investment is made, to provide the firm with updates on its performance and ultimately its sale.

**Investment structure:** The way an investment is set up—to include what is being acquired or invested in, where the investors' money is going in the capital structure (for example, buying equity or debt or both), governance rights accompanying the investment, and the tax features of the investment (for example, the likely tax rates applicable when distributions are made to investors). The major features of the transaction are covered in the investment structure.

**Key employees:** Key employees are individuals who are critical to the investment-making capacity and operation of a private equity firm. Without these individuals, a private equity firm may be prohibited from making key investment decisions for the funds it manages, such as initiating new investments. The idea is that private equity is a people business, and investors are backing the most important people who run the firm on their behalf. The legal agreement between investors and a fund will contain a clause, called a key employee clause (historically, a "key man" clause), that contains this protection for investors. Typically, the key employees are founders, if still at the firm, and a handful of the most senior partners. If key employees leave, the firm may be able to update the key employee clause with individuals who will take the place of the original key employees—with the consent of investors—so the investors can decide whether to back these individuals with their money.

**Lending bank:** A commercial bank that makes loans to companies, businesses, and individuals.

**Leverage:** Debt used by a company or business to finance its operations, or used by investors (or a private equity firm on their behalf) to multiply the purchasing power of money to invest and to amplify investment returns. A private equity investment will use debt to enhance the performance of the deal for investors.

**Leveraged buyout:** The acquisition of a target company or business by (for example) a private equity fund partly using debt to finance the deal. Typically, at least half (and often over seventy percent) of the money used to finance the deal is borrowed, with the rest coming from investors in the fund. A leveraged buyout is the standard way that a private equity fund will buy a target, then seek to improve it through portfolio management and ultimately sell it to make profit.

**Material adverse change:** A change in circumstances that significantly impairs or reduces the value of a company or business that (for example) a private equity fund has agreed to buy. The legal agreement between the fund and target (or its seller) may contain a MAC clause that permits the parties to walk away from the deal before it has been completed. Similarly, the legal agreement between the fund and the Wall Street banks who have agreed to raise high-yield bonds to finance the acquisition may contain a MAC clause to cancel the commitment of the banks to underwrite the financing. Typically, a MAC clause is effective when it protects parties in the agreement against the risk of major unforeseen negative events whose impact is long-term or at least of significant duration, not a short-term blip. Often, disputes over MAC clauses are the subject of litigation.

**Money good:** When an investment is described as being "money good," that implies that the money invested will be paid back and the investment is (or will end up being) worth at least as much money as was put into it (if not with an investment return as well).

**Operating business (also operating company or operating enterprise):** A business that is active in selling products or services to customers or clients. An operating business is different from a dormant business (one that is shut down) or a holding entity (one whose function is to own other companies). When we think about a private equity fund acquiring a business, we are talking about that business having active operations.

**Order book (as in "order book of revenues"):** For a company or business where customers place orders for products or services, the order book is a list of these orders. It can be helpful to build a picture of expected revenues—assuming that the orders are not canceled, are fulfilled, and that customers pay for them. A growing order book can indicate rising demand from customers, whereas a weakening order book can indicate falling demand. The order book is an early indicator of the likely revenues for the company or business, and can serve as an early-warning system if demand is collapsing.

**Passive investing (as in passive vs. active asset management):** Passive investing involves a relatively low amount of buying and selling within the investment portfolio. In contrast, active investing requires a hands-on approach, typically by an asset management firm such as a private equity firm. Passive investing often involves buying index funds, mutual funds, or ETFs with a buy-and-hold mentality. Investors who adopt this passive approach look to participate in the upward trajectory of corporate profits and cash flow over time, accepting that sharp corrections can occur in the financial markets but aiming to ride them out. In contrast, active investing relies on the judgment of the people hired to make the investment decisions, such as when to buy and sell, and the quality and depth of their analysis. Passive investing is much cheaper for investors than active investing because there are no investment professionals selecting individual companies or businesses to invest in, and oversight of the investments is much more limited. If passive investing produces a superior investment return than a given active investor over a similar time horizon, despite being cheaper for investors, there is a strong reason to suggest that the active asset manager in question is underperforming.

Permanent capital (or perpetual capital): A permanent or perpetual capital vehicle is a type of investment whereby the money put in is available for a theoretically unlimited time. Unlike a private equity fund, in which the money from investors is available to invest for a limited time, such as ten years, and is drawn down over time, in a permanent capital vehicle the money is always available once it has been raised. The "always on" availability of permanent capital breaks the onerous cycle of fundraising that is found in private equity because firms do not return to the investors every few years to raise money. And, of course, once a permanent capital vehicle is raised, the private equity firm managing it can charge fees and invest the money in the vehicle forever—in theory.

**Portfolio management:** The work on an investment, such as a company or business acquired in a leveraged buyout by a private equity fund, done by the investment professionals together with the senior management team of the enterprise to increase the value of the enterprise. Successful portfolio management can help increase profit—and make the enterprise more valuable.

**Private capital:** A general term for investments that are not publicly traded like stocks and bonds. Private capital includes private equity and the other investment strategies mentioned in this book, such as credit, real estate, and infrastructure. These investments are harder to sell immediately for cash than publicly traded investments, and they are also more complex and can carry more risk. Because of these factors, private capital investments generate higher and more consistent investment returns over time than publicly traded investments, whose valuations can be more volatile. (At least, that's the intention.) When these investments fail or underperform, they have the disadvantages of being less liquid and making lower investment returns than, for example, just buying and holding a basket of well-performing stocks. Private capital investments are also more expensive for investors because of the fees and expenses charged by asset management firms to actively manage them.

**Private equity:** An investment in a company or business where the aim is to grow and improve the enterprise before exiting at a profit. The investment is typically made through a fund, called a private equity fund, or another structure set up by a private equity firm to invest money. Private equity investments generally involve the fund assuming control of an enterprise, or at least having significant influence over it. A private equity investment is usually made by acquiring or funding a stake in, or all of, an enterprise, but it can also involve other methods, such as buying the distressed debt of a good enterprise temporarily in financial trouble.

**Realization:** A realization is money paid out to investors, for example in a private equity fund. The source of the realization will be income or capital gain from one or more investments in the fund. The total amount of realizations during the life of an investment will equal the total money paid out to investors, for example distributions of income over time plus a capital gain when the investment is sold.

**Shadow banks:** A general term for financial services organizations that provide lending similar to traditional banks but do not take deposits and are not regulated in the same way as traditional banks. Private equity firms are often called shadow banks because of their credit-investing activities, such as the direct arrangement of loans with companies or businesses who wish to borrow money.

**SPAC:** A special purpose acquisition company, set up to raise money from investors through an initial public offering (IPO) for the sole purpose of buying or merging with an existing company. It's a "blank check" shell that holds investors' money and has to complete a deal within a set time frame (e.g., two years) or return the money. For private equity firms, SPACs are an additional means of making and selling out of investments.

**Target:** The enterprise or asset being considered as a potential investment. Typically, targets that a private equity firm considers are companies or businesses where the private equity fund that the firm manages may acquire a stake in or control of the enterprise. The fund can also target the debt issued by the enterprise instead of buying the equity.

**Two and Twenty:** A standard fee arrangement in the private equity industry. Private equity firms charge investors both a management fee and a performance fee. The management fee is typically an annual fee of two percent of assets under management. The performance fee, also known as the incentive fee, is typically twenty percent of profits made from investments. The performance fee is often payable only if a hurdle or threshold is met for the investment return. For example, if a given investment makes over eight percent in annual return, then twenty percent of all profit made from the investment is taken as an incentive fee; if the return is less than eight percent, no fee is taken.

**Value creation:** Increasing the value of an investment. For example, for a private equity investment in a company or business, improving the growth and profitability of the enterprise can result in a higher valuation that a new buyer would be willing to pay for the enterprise.

**Warehousing [as in "warehousing assets"]:** Warehousing is when an asset management firm sets up and manages a temporary structure to hold an investment, such as a stake in a company or business, before transferring this investment to a structure that is intended to last for a longer period. For example, when a private equity firm is looking to complete a compelling investment opportunity for its investors that does not fit into its existing funds, it can still secure the deal by setting up a special bespoke vehicle to hold this investment, funded using investors' money. Months after the deal is complete, the firm can transfer the investment to a longer-term structure, such as a new private equity fund intended to be in place for over ten years. During this transfer period to a private equity fund, new investors who did not participate earlier can be brought in.

## About the Author

SACHIN KHAJURIA is a former partner at Apollo, one of the world's largest alternative asset management firms, and is also an investor in funds managed by Blackstone and Carlyle, among other major investment firms. He has twenty-five years of investment and finance experience. Khajuria holds two honors degrees in economics from the University of Cambridge. He lives in New York City and Switzerland.

## About the Type

THIS BOOK was set in Caslon, a typeface first designed in 1722 by William Caslon (1692–1766). Its widespread use by most English printers in the early eighteenth century soon supplanted the Dutch typefaces that had formerly prevailed. The roman is considered a "workhorse" typeface due to its pleasant, open appearance, while the italic is exceedingly decorative.